Champagne
& Self
Loathing

Everything, but not enough

By Suzanne Selvester

Champagne & Self Loathing
Written by
Suzanne Selvester

A catalogue record for this book is available from The
British Library

Published by Hope & Plum Publishing
www.hopeandplum.com

ISBN 9781838030230

For Sean, Ethan and Sam.
My heart, my soul, my love.

Heartfelt thanks to

Hannah Tansley who nailed it with the name of this book while we all scratched our heads trying to think of one.

Elaine Harrison who repeatedly sent the finished manuscript back asking for more. You literally pulled this story from the depths of my soul and I'm forever grateful.

My publisher, Stacey Haber, for believing in me and this book.

My ex-husband for the support and friendship over the years, you've been amazing.

My sons for simply being alive and allowing me the pleasure of being your mother

And finally, to myself. For forgiving my imperfections and inadequacies, and finally learning to love myself unconditionally.

Introduction

If someone told me ten years ago I'd know inner peace, be gloriously happy and realise the meaning of my life, I'd have done anything to achieve it. To know myself completely? To love and accept myself? To live without fear and experience inner peace?

yes please, sign me up

If they'd also told me the price I'd pay, I might not have been as enthusiastic and would have scarpered

fast

in the opposite direction. If I'd known I'd be forced to face unimaginable fear, ingrained into my DNA, confront deep emotional pain that would tear me apart and annihilate every single belief I'd ever held? Even in the darkest moments, I'd still have said yes, a million times for the prize.

My name is Suzanne and that's probably the only thing I was ever certain of growing up in working class Catholic Ireland in the 1970's. I was a girl with dreams, one who questioned the world and demanded answers. At school I'd argue with nuns about the relevance of subjects that were so mind numbing, they'd send me to sleep.

I mean who would ever need to use theorems in their life?
Really!

I was a rebel and pushed against what I thought were ridiculous rules, set by strict catholic nuns, running a convent school. On top of that, I challenged authority everywhere I went. A strict

5

policy of staying on school grounds during lunchtime was completely unreasonable, I'd tell myself as I scaled the six foot wall to go home for my lunch everyday.

I was never caught.

However...

and this is the root of the whole story

I was also raised on a steady diet of fear, guilt and shame. Predominantly by the school, the church, my working class environment and my childhood program that was fueled by fear. I did have a lot of love in my life, but it didn't counteract my ability to doubt myself at every turn and I developed an irrational idea that I was somehow unworthy of happiness. Just being myself never felt enough, I had to impress people, I had to shine to breath and as a result became the ultimate people pleaser.

be what everyone else needs and forget about you.
It's only your life after all!

A tiny part of me resisted this, it was buried deep in the trenches of my soul, beneath the people pleasing and it knew there was more to me. It wanted more for me and from a very young age it pushed me to know who I was and why I was alive. Of course I didn't understand any of this and thought there was something wrong with me. Constantly feeling torn between a strong urge to know myself and a deep rooted need to fit in, resulting in me lingering on the edge of my life, almost getting what I wanted, but not quite.

The edge of happiness; a place from which I watched the lives of others and yearned for the happiness I perceived them to have.

6

tell me again why everyone is happier than me?

The edge of financial security; deeply affected by my working class background, I made money my goal in life and when I got it, I couldn't enjoy it because I constantly worried about losing it. The edge of peace, absolutely craving peace I never felt and telling myself when this,

> *I got skinny, had more money and a new car*

or that

> *I got skinny, had the latest Chanel handbag*
> *and a new house*

happened, I'd find it. Most importantly of all, I lived on the edge of love, swooning and daydreaming about true love. I'd imagine what my soulmate looked like while fantasising about our perfect relationship. All the while being secretly terrified I'd never find it...

> *because I didn't deserve it*

Unable to allow my life to naturally unfold, I took action.

> *subconscious control-freak, action,*
> *but I didn't know that at the time*

I created an illusion powerful enough to convince me I had it all.

> *and shut up the internal disquiet for five minutes*

I fell in love, married a great guy, had three beautiful kids and a fantastic lifestyle. That should be enough. I made it, so why did I always feel like something was missing? Why did I compare my life to everyone else's and why did it seem as though they all had what I desperately wanted? Everyone seemed more content and more in love with their partners than I was. They had

in my mind

beautiful homes with more family time, better cars, nicer holidays, more peace and much happier lives. My life seemed bland in comparison.

why couldn't I have what they had?

Of course, I did have it, the material things anyway, but I couldn't see it. To fill the void in me, I needed more and that meant more of everything! I was consumed with wanting more, unable to appreciate what I already had. Continually projecting my life forward, I'd tell myself everything I wanted,

no, everything I needed to be happy

was on the other side of tomorrow and systematically lived in a future that didn't exist.

On the outside everything looked perfect; I had a champagne lifestyle.

and boy did I drink enough of it

My home was actually beautiful,

it just wasn't as nice as the neighbours'

my husband was successful,

just not as successful as my friend's husband

the kids went to private school,

there were better ones in London

we had five holidays a year, travelling first class

ok, you've got me on that one, that was great

and I did as much shopping as a girl could dream about.

I was always too fat to really enjoy it

On the inside however, my self-loathing ripped me apart and the disquiet I'd always felt began to gain momentum.

Then one day, just after my 35th birthday, it broke free and the shit hit the fan. Reading the first five chapters of a random book, my illusion came crashing down around me and I gained clarity that took my breath away. A flash of brutal honesty that allowed me to see beyond the facade I'd created, and I was lambasted by it. I don't know why it was this book at this particular time, but as I read it, I shattered into a million pieces. The book was about love, a love so pure it triggered an extreme reaction and even though I knew it was fiction, it was my catalyst and my heart sank to my feet as I realised two things.

The first: **I didn't know love**.

what? I didn't know love?

Apart from the unconditional love I felt as a mother, I didn't feel anything else.

as in nothing, nada

Until then, I hadn't questioned my feelings for my husband. We had our ups and downs like everyone else, but in a second, I knew something very important was missing from our relationship. He was a good man and I did love him, but not the way I should after ten years of marriage. I felt alone, unloved, unsafe and unsupported, I just hadn't noticed before. I hadn't noticed that everything had become hard, hard to communicate, hard to have fun, hard to love and when I tried to remember the last time I'd felt anything similar to joy, I couldn't. How had I become so emotionally shut down?

The second realisation:

and this was a killer

Who the fuck am I? The fear that followed this realisation is something I will remember for the rest of my life. Unable to breathe, I tumbled headfirst into a pit of despair as I tried to remember what I wanted from my life. What my likes and dislikes were, what was my favourite colour, my favourite flower, my favourite food? Where had my hopes and dreams gone? I was 35 years old and so engrossed in my own perfect illusion, that I'd disappeared into it. I'd suppressed my feelings for years, hidden who I was

even from myself

and managed to convince myself that everything was amazing, when clearly it wasn't.

The illusion shattered and a new reality began. I found myself on the most extraordinary journey of my life, a journey of self discovery that would take me to hell and back. I'd be forced to face my deepest fears and finally accept who I was, but not before resisting every step of the way.

I'd be dragged kicking and screaming towards self realisation

I wanted to stay in the pain of being disconnected from my true self. It seemed easier and pain was an old friend, a familiar confidant that I didn't want to let go. I was an expert at feeling unworthy, unsafe and unloved. I was well practiced in extreme self-loathing and would tell myself everyday I was fat, ugly or stupid. To change that meant to change who I was and that terrified me.

In spite of that however, something bigger forced me onto this path and I had no choice but to start walking. Searching for answers everywhere, I read millions of self-help books,

more like thousands

attended course after course,

some good, some shit

and felt like I'd die if I didn't find myself. 'Who am I?' became my biggest question and eventually… I found the answer. The peace I dreamed about became available to me and my life had meaning. I worked it out, I was living my absolute truth, was self realised, knew my purpose and felt happy for the first time in years. Of course it was then that the Universe clobbered me with the hardest lesson of all. A lesson so profound it would almost destroy me and force me to surrender completely.

This is my story and I had to share it. It's a story of love and transformation, not just romantic love, but all aspects of love. I wrote it as if no one would ever read it and at times could barely type the words as shame and humiliation poured onto these pages. It's my journey and it might be your journey. My lessons might be your lessons. Each one has shaped me into the woman I am today, a woman whose sense of self is never again up for negotiation because through it all:

> I have peace. I speak my truth. I live and love wholeheartedly. I own my fear, embrace my madness and nurture my vulnerability. I live my life with unbridled passion and I laugh easily at the mistakes I make. I finally found myself and I finally love myself

1: The End

The cure for pain is in the pain.

- ***Rumi***

As I sat frozen in panic, looking at the two pieces of paper in my husband's hand, I felt like I was going to throw up. Two white A4 sheets, one listing 'everything I was doing wrong' in our marriage and the other completely blank. This was it, his ultimatum and his breaking point. As if in slow motion, he lifted one hand and waved the first sheet, "We can do this the hard way Suzanne and discuss everything on this list or," waving the other one said "we can do it the easy way and end this marriage right now." My first thought apart from being sick was, 'oh fuck, here it is.' I'd known this was coming for quite some time and was hoping our problems would just go away and disappear, but here it was staring me in the face and all I could do was stare back at it, incapable of responding.

Earlier that day he'd unexpectedly called to say he was coming home early and wanted to talk to me and I trembled on the end of the line, terrified of what was about to happen.

my head was still firmly dug in the sand

Business had demanded most of his time lately and we barely saw each other. For him to make time to talk, meant something big and I was shit scared. I knew we were on borrowed time in our marriage. My anxiety was through the roof every single day and even though I wanted to talk about our problems,

I really did

I was too afraid to bring it up so I avoided it like the plague.

1

We'd been steadily deteriorating for the past two years and at times it felt like we hated each other, but even in those times, a small part of me hoped we'd find our way through it. We'd both been raised in families where our parents were still together, so having what was perceived to be a successful marriage

happy or not

was important to us.

When I hung up, I tried very hard not to hyperventilate, but my stomach was churning and my nerves were shot to bits. I fed my sons early, got them bathed and ready for daddy to put them to bed. My three gorgeous boys who kept me sane through the threat of my world being blown apart. Sean was ten, Ethan was seven and Sammie was five and they were amazing. I thought they didn't know what was happening, but they did. Sean had definitely worked out something was very wrong, because as much as we tried to hide it, he heard his mother screaming like a banshee, witnessed the tears and tantrums and could feel the tension in the house.

When Kevin arrived home, he barely looked at me and went straight upstairs to spend time with his kids. He read them bedtime stories and I could hear playful laughter coming from their rooms as I sat trembling in the lounge, with a big glass of white wine and an even bigger sense of foreboding.

I was absolutely shitting myself
and wanted to run, very far away

Twenty minutes later when he came downstairs, I was a nervous wreck and completely unprepared for what was about to take

2

place, even though I knew it had to happen. He'd been sleeping in the spare room for six months and our relationship was limping along, fractured in so many places. Our marriage had to end, but I was paralysed by fear and completely unable to face it.

He didn't bother with small talk or light discussion. He just produced the two pieces of paper and as I looked at him dressed immaculately in a business suit, I wondered if this was just like a business meeting for him.

next on the agenda is.... my divorce!

He seemed to be in complete control as he went on to say, "Page one is a list of everything you're doing to make me unhappy," then pausing,

as if for effect

said "Page two is blank and the end of our marriage."

Instantly it struck me how he'd only focused on what I was doing wrong. There was no mention of his behaviour or his contribution to the problems in our marriage; but my terror and fucked up perception that I was always in the wrong, meant I ignored it. I didn't want this...yet I did. I was terrified, but attentive, knowing this was my way out, but did I really want a way out? What if I was alone forever?

Spinster Suzanne

What if I couldn't do it without him? What if he didn't take care of me financially?

3

did that mean I'd be poor again?

Where would we live?

on the streets?

The voice in my head was relentless as it sent me into a frenzy of fear.

"Make a choice Suzanne," he prompted.

no I don't want to, please leave me alone

"Because I won't live like this anymore." We'd nearly split up six months earlier but I lost my nerve and convinced

begged

him to try again for the sake of the kids. This time I knew it was over. We could talk about the problems on his list but what was the point? We'd already discussed them and I already felt like a big fat failure. I knew I was lazy, hopeless, disorganised, unaffectionate and ungrateful.

he told me so all the time

I also knew I could never be what he needed me to be, so I took a deep breath, closed my eyes and nodded towards the blank piece of paper. I made my choice.

It might have been one of the only times I witnessed raw emotion on my husband's face throughout our whole marriage. He was always in control, no matter what, but now he shook his head

4

from side to side and with a look of utter devastation and began to cry.

shit, what now?

I was absolutely horrified to be the cause of this, so I cried as well. The thought of hurting him was one of the main reasons I'd tried to make the marriage work, but I never thought it would come to this. I thought he'd be pissed off at me, call me a slag, walk out and slam the door. Watching him sob his heart out, tore me apart and I was devastated. My tears however were a combination of many things: hurt, sadness, fear and relief. Having danced around it for nearly two years, we'd finally faced it.

well...he had anyway

Admitting it was over,

and after all the crying

we were able to be more open and honest with each other and both agreed this wasn't love; this wasn't the way a marriage should be. We'd somehow gone from loving each other to emotionally kicking the shit out of each other every single day. The mutual disrespect we had was shocking and a huge distance had grown between us with all intimacy and affection long gone.

God, I missed being kissed

Ironically we talked more that night than we had in a long time. We agreed on a six month trial separation, Kevin would look for somewhere else to live and we'd see how it went. I assured him his relationship with his sons would be whatever he wanted it to

5

be and vowed never to use them as a weapon. Our finances and other details could be decided at a later date and that was it, the deed was done. Our 12 year wedding anniversary was the following week and we didn't quite make it.

I might have held out for the gift
but it was only silk and linen

We finished the wine,

I did

gave each other a hug and went to our separate beds.

As I lay in bed, I was swamped with emotions. For two years I'd known my marriage was over, but I didn't have the courage to finish it. I'd talk myself into it, then talk myself out of it. I'd convince myself our problems were all in my head. 'SHUT UP SUZANNE,' I'd shout at myself on a regular basis, ridiculing myself for wanting more. Mocking my thoughts of soulmate love,

that probably didn't exist

of happiness, peace and purpose that were just unavailable to me.

get over it

I'd unknowingly allowed emotions such as dread, panic and anxiety be my normal state of mind and was unwilling to consider anything else being possible for me.

Now everything was possible - I just had to get past my soul crushing fear, the driving force in my life. I'd just turned thirty eight, I had three children, hadn't worked in over ten years and on top of that, I was in the middle of a huge identity crisis that saw panic and anxiety

and madness

consume me on a daily basis. What was next? What kind of job could I get? What kind of life would I have? Although I was bombarded by these thoughts, a small part of me felt calm and I clung to that. The hardest part was done, the break had been made and on that thought, I fell asleep for the first time in over two years without anxiety and fear at the forefront of my mind.

Over breakfast we told the boys that daddy was going to live in a new house and they would stay there sometimes. They knew what that meant and although a little confused, were excited at the prospect of having new bedrooms. Sean figured it out straight away, but his brothers were still too young to completely understand and I was consumed with guilt for putting them through this.

stay calm, it will be okay

I played at being lighthearted, but I was dying inside. Telling them turned out to be easier than we expected though. They seemed to take it in their stride, nod their heads and go back to watching Peppa Pig.

Within a week, Kevin made plans to move out and I helped him. We found a house for him to rent about 15 minutes away. It was cute and comfortable and I knew the boys would like it there. Three short weeks later when he left, the tension I hadn't known

7

I was holding onto, left with him. The dread of him coming home from work was gone. I no longer had to rush around at six o'clock to make sure the house was clean,

or be called a lazy bitch

or brace myself for whatever argument was coming that night.

usually no milk or my shit being all over his side of the bedroom

I hadn't realised how heavy it was, until it was gone.

The following weekend when he came to get the boys, I completely lost it. There were no words to describe how I felt, watching him drive away with my children, smiling and waving at me, their cute little faces excited at the prospect of seeing daddy's new house. I closed the front door, slid down it, sat on the floor and wailed. My anxiety burned through me as I thought. 'What the fuck am I supposed to do now?'

drink wine?

For the first time in over ten years my kids weren't with me and I couldn't move for fear. I sat reflecting on the past 12 years of my marriage and realised I hadn't felt loved by my husband in a very long time. In the beginning it was wonderful and we were in love, but I couldn't remember the last time I'd felt that way. Had he stopped loving me or had I stopped loving him? When Kevin told me he loved me, which he did until things became really bad, I simply didn't believe him. How could he love me? How could anyone love me? In my mind I was unlovable.

8

I thought about my relationship with my kids and how unhappy I'd been in front of them these past few years. Had they noticed? Did they think I was a miserable, *drunk* mummy? I adored my kids, but I was also deeply entrenched in my unhappiness and suddenly terrified they noticed. Wrecked by feelings of failure, to add to that, I now had no power over their weekend. What were they eating or what time would they go to bed? Still wailing like a banshee, I eventually got off the floor, had a bath and drowned my misery in a bottle of wine.

maybe it was two

I told myself I could do this; I was strong and I was going to find a way to continue, because I had no other choice.

My life was in free-fall and I was now officially living my deepest fears: the fear of being alone, the fear of having no money, and the fear of failing. Amid it all I remembered a quote by Winston Churchill. He said, "When you're in hell, just keep going."

oh piss off Winston

but he was right, what else could I do?

I didn't realise at the time I was about to embark on a life changing journey. My separation finally pushed me toward something I'd avoided since reading that book two years previously, but I never could have comprehended the path ahead. I didn't know such a path existed. I didn't know such pain existed. All I knew was there had to be more to my life than the unhappiness and anxiety I lived with on a daily basis and I wanted to find it.

I wanted to understand myself more, but to do that I had to go back and unravel my past. Find out why I felt the way I did about myself, how I'd become this version of me and what had happened to make me feel so unworthy of love.

2: A Childhood Program

My religion is very simple, my religion is kindness.
- ***Dalai Lama***

Growing up in 1970s Catholic Ireland wasn't ideal for a girl like me. The church was a huge part of our lives and the all-girls school I attended was run by strict Catholic nuns. Mass on Sunday was a must and even though I hated it, I couldn't miss it because first thing on Monday morning we were thoroughly quizzed on what gospel was read. God help us if we didn't know.

School life for me was generally miserable and I can't seem to remember a single nun being nice or kind to me. Maybe one or two were kinder than the others, but mostly, they were strict, hard women who rarely smiled. Our first lesson was fear. Fear of these nuns with their harsh expressions, bamboo canes and steel rulers. Fear of God, the devil, our teachers, ourselves, our ambitions and basically anything positive that might happen in our lives.

fear rules!

The next lesson was shame. I used to think it was guilt but later realised it was shame, something much more destructive. We were regularly made to feel ashamed of ourselves, our bodies, our desires, our pride if we achieved too much, our laziness if we achieved too little. A school day could quickly turn into a horror show if you were targeted by a nun. "Who owns this piece of work?" Sister would say, holding the copybook high for the class to see. She knew exactly who owned it, but liked to display her power. Immediately we'd sink down in our chairs, dread quickly spreading through the classroom as we realised whoever owned it, was about to be humiliated and ridiculed in front of everyone.

There were star pupils who shined brightly and were highly favoured, but the rest of us were considered lazy and incompetent by Sisters who expected academic perfection. Being told you're a wicked, incompetent girl on a daily basis takes root and before long, you start to believe it. Throughout my whole school life, I thought I was exactly that, but I wasn't... I was actually very bright, just completely uninterested in their methods of torture...

I mean teaching

Another lesson quickly learned was pain, something you got used to when schooled by nuns in the 1970s. The bamboo cane and steel ruler were their weapons of choice and we were regularly assaulted with them. The boys attending the Christian Brothers school weren't so lucky either and usually got hit with a belt, a paddle or a fist by these so called men of God.

ahem..child abuse anyone?

At the time we didn't realise it was abuse. We just thought life was hard, nothing came easy and we were born to live a life of penance, misery and sin. On our final day we'd get to face the judgement of God at the gates of heaven blah, blah, blah. Of course we believed every word like a faithful flock of sheep.

Baaaa

12

Our parents believed it and in fact were so indoctrinated by the church they never questioned any of it; regularly going to mass, they respected the church and passed it down to their children.

It always felt wrong to me, I was like a fish out of water and hated their rules, which meant I spent a lot of time in front of a particularly nasty headmistress called Sister Lorencia. With a look of delight she'd deliver ten lashes to each of my palms using her famed bamboo cane and if I made a sound, I'd get ten more.

definitely child abuse.

I was probably about 10 years old and in agony as each lash felt like fire, but it was acceptable back then. Now as a mother of three boys, if any were disciplined in this way, I'd call the police.

My family life was good, my parents were working class folks who lived a working class lifestyle and we lived on a road full of kids. Our house had belonged to my grandmother and was in an old neighbourhood where everyone knew who you were. We had a great big park at the end of our back garden which meant we could disappear for hours - and often did. We'd build a den in the bushes or catch bees in jam jars and no one ever worried about us being gone all day. "They'll come home when they're hungry," my mother would say, and she was right, we did.

From a young age I was the curious one in the family.

Or the pain in the ass, depending on how you look at it

I questioned everything and always wanted my mother to take me here or there, a new dance class, a certain park, a holiday. Bombarding her with questions, I wanted to know why the grass was green and the sky was blue. I was also a child who liked my own company and spent a lot of time in my treehouse, at the top of a great big sycamore tree in our back garden. I built it myself with two planks of wood, a blanket, a couple of cushions and a lot of love. It was perfect and it was mine. I'd lay in it looking up at the sky, wondering about life and daydreaming about fame and fortune.

When I was nine, my best friend was 27 and the most beautiful woman I knew. Her name was Margaret, she lived three doors away and I'd visit her everyday after school to tell her all about my adventures. When she eventually got married, I asked my mother to take me to University Church on St Stephen's Green to see her. Years later, Margaret told me that when she came back from her honeymoon, I declared, aged nine, that one day I was going to get married in the exact same church.

I did, but that's for later

As well as being a dreamer, I was also the sick child in the family. Asthma, allergies and a damaged liver made St James's Hospital in Dublin my second home and I liked it that way. The doctors made a fuss of me while trying to figure out what was wrong and I felt so important. I got lots of attention from my mother, loads of time off school and being sick gave me the excuse I needed to feel different from my family and friends. I wanted to be considered special and loved talking about my illnesses.

where shall I start?

I'd use my ailments as a way to make me appear more interesting to others, something I carried through to my adult life.

14

My mother would say I was her cross to bear. She worried about me more than her other kids and we were very close. I loved her so much, she made me feel safe and I always wanted to be around my mother. Her lightheartedness as she'd sing and dance around the kitchen with our dog, Lady, thrilled me. Her ability to cook up a storm from what seemed like an empty cupboard or fridge was amazing. If visitors came she would always say, "There may be no food in the fridge, but it will always be on the table," as she'd sprint across the road to the local shop for supplies.

like an Olympian

I didn't know it then, but I was also deeply affected by her pain. Her life wasn't always easy and it weighed heavy on me. I sometimes felt it was my responsibility to make sure she was happy, to make life a bit easier for her and was always looking for ways to do that. Our working class status meant we didn't go too far from home and summer holidays were usually a trip to Wicklow to a friend's mobile home. While there, my mother would take us to the beach,

she was such a star

and my father would go to his favourite place.

le pub

Even if we weren't on holiday, my dad spent a lot of his time in the pub while my mother stayed at home, taking care of us. When I was very young, I remember him coming home some Friday nights from work

usually via the pub and usually drunk

15

with bags of sweets in his pockets, lots of attention for us kids and being playful and fun. I loved those nights with my dad when he'd give his winnings from the horse racing to my mother and we were all happy.

Other times though, he'd come home with nothing at all, having spent his wages in the pub or having lost it on the horses. My mother would cry and I hated it, deeply resenting my father for putting her through this. I'd sit on the stairs,

with tummy ache

unable to stop myself from listening to their arguments and worry about paying the bills or buying food for the family. It was then that my anxiety was born and worrying would be something that came very easily to me later in my life.

Generally, I didn't like my dad very much. He was cranky and was always giving out to us. I'd sometimes wonder why he preferred being in the pub, instead of at home with his family, but as time went on, I preferred it that way. It meant I had my mother all to myself,

I did share her with my brother and sister,
but she was mostly mine

One day when I was about 12 old, my father took redundancy from work and overnight my whole life changed. My mother got a full time job and my dad stayed at home to take care of us. Rather than skipping home from school to my mother, I dreaded going home to my dad.

His impatience,

16

pissed me off. Taking care of us, making us dinner or helping with our homework pissed him off.

we were so alike.

He loved us, I never doubted that, he just wasn't very good at affection and although my older brother and sister weren't bothered by it, I was. I was a child who needed more, who needed to be told or shown I was loved.

Please tell me how amazing I am, please tell me you love me.

I wanted my parents to tell me every single day,

twice a day, 10 times a day

how much they loved me and how proud of me they were, but I never got that. They didn't openly express their emotions and I yearned for it, the feeling of emotional deprivation already in me and something I'd feel for a very long time.

In my teenage years, I was more in control so going home from school wasn't a problem. At 3.15pm, when the school bell rang, I'd go to my best friend Tara's house. Tara's parents were friends with my parents, we were like family and most days I went to play with all the babies,

and to nick 50 pence pieces
from her dad's MASSIVE jar full of them

She had five considerably younger brothers and sisters, her house was wonderfully chaotic and I loved being there. I'd stay until I knew my mother was back from work, then I'd go home to see her.

Avoiding alone time with grumpy pants

Another very significant person in my life was my neighbour and kindred soul, Claire. Claire lived two doors away and became my new best friend when Margaret moved to Canada. She was even older at fifty but the age gap didn't matter to me, she was like a second mother and I loved her. Separated from her husband, she lived alone with her two dogs, Tarry

little shit

and Shanta

swoon

Her home was warm and cosy, with red gabardine curtains, a roaring coal fire and I felt safe there. If I wasn't at Tara's house, I was usually at Claire's.

I'd pop in on the way home from school and we'd sit by the fire talking about love, life and romance. Oh how we loved romance.

Sometimes I'd go to the shop across the road to get her milk, bread and cigarettes,

of which I'd nick a couple

18

while she made the tea. Then I'd give her a rundown of all the drama in my life. She'd listen, laugh at my tales and often shake her head saying, "Chicken,

a term of endearment in Ireland

I wish I could put my old head on your young shoulders." I didn't know what she meant until later in my life but as Oscar Wilde puts it, 'youth is wasted on the young.' I was unable to see past the problems of being fifteen years old and trying to figure everything out. Claire would help me mash through it, giving me advice without judgement, but of course I never listened, usually doing the opposite and causing myself more drama.

Claire was one of the most important people in my life growing up.

I regularly thank the Universe for her

She was and still is a beautiful woman who listened to me without ever making me feel irrelevant. She knew every detail of my life, because I kept nothing from her. We laughed so much together and even today when I visit Ireland, I pop in and see her. Now in her 80s, she's still rocking it. Marie was my other 50 year old friend. I did have friends my own age, but liked being around older people. Marie and Claire were great friends and I was part of that friendship.

During my final year in school, I spent most of my time 'on the hop'

a term for bunking off school in Ireland.

19

My mother left for work early and my dad didn't pay much attention, so I'd get ready for school as normal, then go to Marie's house and hang out there until 3.15pm. Marie took care of her grandchildren during the day which meant she was up early and always home, so I'd wait until her husband Christy left for work, then slip in the back door. We'd play with the babies and talk about life, love and romance while drinking tea and eating cakes. She tried to get me to go to school,

just go Suzanne, even a couple of days a week!!!

but she eventually gave up trying because she knew I wouldn't go.

There was a very good reason I got away with being absent from school without a hard knock on our front door by a somewhat pissed off nun.

wasting time chasing after truants seriously annoyed them.

A couple of months before my 17th birthday, I was diagnosed with a brain tumor.

Having experienced strange symptoms for quite some time, I'd been in and out of St James Hospital for test after test and when the day finally came to get the results, I sat in the doctor's office with my mother. Obviously delighted with yet another excuse to be out of class, that was until the doctor delivered the diagnosis. "You have a brain tumor," she said and I nearly fell off my chair.

What? Is she joking? A brain tumor?

How could I have a brain tumour? I felt absolutely fine. She explained I had a benign brain tumour and I'd probably be infertile as a result of it.

Wicked news - my dream of being a mother
just washed down the drain.

Rather than having surgery to remove it, I was prescribed strong medication to hopefully reduce it in size. It made me throw up every morning. This resulted in me missing a lot of school initially, but... as my body adapted, I felt better. My parents knew this, but the school didn't and taking full advantage of the situation, I didn't tell them and bunked off.

When I got over the initial shock of having a tumour and no future babies, I realised I had something else that made me different and even more interesting.

jackpot! a brain tumour!
this was solid gold,
I'm really sick kind of stuff

I'd regularly talk about it, relishing in people's reactions when I'd very casually drop it into a conversation. Never for a second did I consider the health implications or the possible consequences of it, I just enjoyed having another reason to feel different and special.

my need to fit in hadn't emerged yet.

When I turned up at school for my end of school exams, my classmates and teachers were surprised to see me because they thought I'd left. I figured I'd come this far, so might as well take the exams and smiled as I strolled in and sat at my desk. Being clever gave me an advantage and I could have been a really good student if I'd tried, but I found school so horribly boring. I thought there had to be more to life than learning about shit that would never be of any use to me.

Over the years I'd debated with several nuns on the benefits

or not

of algebra. They didn't like me very much because I asked uncomfortable questions which they never answered. When I got five honours and two passes,

a decent result back then

Sister Pat, the school principal, took me into her office. "Well done Suzanne," she said, "now imagine what you could have achieved if you'd actually come to school."

ah, busted.

She knew I was milking the tumour but I didn't care, I hated school. I'd watch those nuns going from the convent to the school and back again, only to repeat it the next day and the day after that. I thought it must feel suffocating. The repetitiveness of their lives frightened me so much and I swore I'd never live that way, routine and convention becoming two of my biggest fears.

3: First Love

Love Does Not Want or Fear Anything.
- Eckhart Tolle

He was the most beautiful boy I'd ever seen and by my last year of bunking school, I'd known the agony of unrequited love for almost three years. When I was fifteen, I set my sights on him and chased after him for six months, determined he'd be mine. When he finally asked me out, my life was complete. He was seventeen and I thought he was so sophisticated. I was thrilled to have such a clever and ambitious boyfriend. My first real boyfriend. For almost a year I was in heaven until one day out of the blue, he broke it off with me and I experienced my first broken heart.

His family owned the butchers shop across the road from my house and when I was in hot pursuit, I'd stand at my front door watching him at work behind the counter, willing him to look my way. He of course would and we'd have a staring match. I never averted my eyes, confident in my claim on him and convinced he was already in love with me. It was only a matter of time before he'd ask me out and when we were invited to the same 21st birthday party, we slow danced to Michael Jackson. He asked me on a date and we were official.

I finally had him and I wasn't letting him go.

Absolutely mad about him, I straight away became the girl who disappeared into the boy she loved; we were boyfriend/girlfriend,

as in happy ever after, marriage, kids and so on

23

so I only wanted to be with him and no one else mattered.

Friends? Who were they?

My boyfriend needed to be happy and I was the sole source of that happiness so whatever he needed from me, he got and I would drop everything

and everyone

to be by his side. Of course he was often unavailable, busy with work or at home with his family and I couldn't understand why he didn't want to spend every single second of every single day with me, like I did with him.

WTF? he actually had a life without me?
I hated the thought of it.

A week before my sixteenth birthday, I lost my virginity to him. Having talked it through with Claire, Marie and all my same age girlfriends, we agreed the time was right. I'd been with him for over seven months and was ready to hand over the V card. His parents were away for the weekend, my girlfriends covered for me and I went to his house for the night.

excited beyond anything I'd ever experienced

When he led me to his bedroom, I thought I'd die with desire for him, but when he started taking off my clothes, it became awkward and weird and I felt absolutely mortified. Suddenly realising I had to be naked in front of him, my confidence drained away and my self-consciousness wrenched up. I hated how I looked and could barely move with embarrassment. He was going to see my fat arse and small boobs and never want to see me again.

My arse wasn't fat and my boobs were cute

Thankfully he turned out the light and we got into bed to do the business. However, my excitement swiftly evaporated when all I experienced was a bit of pushing and shoving, a sharp pain and a few grunts, then he rolled off me.

eh...was that it and ouch, it hurt

It was his first time too, so he didn't really know what to do. There was no intimacy, no loving connection and no conversation. It turned out to be a very quick, very painful experience and afterwards he kissed me goodnight, propped up his pillows, turned over and was out cold.

WTF?

He worked such long hours, was always knackered and I was left lying alone in the dark at 10pm thinking what the fuck has just happened.

with him snoring beside me

I'd imagined us staying up all night talking about our hopes and dreams, enjoying a midnight picnic and laying in each other's arms, but none of that happened and I was sick with disappointment.

Of course I talked myself out of it by the next morning and convinced myself it had been perfect, everything I'd ever dreamed off.

That's what I told my girlfriends anyway. I already had a knack for convincing myself and others of what I wanted to believe, completely unwilling to consider anything other than my glossed-over, rose-tinted version of life.

A few weeks later, he took me to my prom and I was once again thrilled to show him off.

> *my boyfriend has a car, actually, a jeep.*
> *does yours?*

I was proud as punch with my handsome boyfriend. We had dinner with all my friends and just when the party was getting started, he asked if we could go for a drive.

> *eh...what?*

Being doe-eyed in love with him, I of course agreed and left the party. When he drove to The Hellfire club in Dublin, I knew exactly what was on his mind and we of course had sex in the car park, then he fell asleep and I sat in the passenger seat alone waiting for him to wake up. By the time he did, it was two am and I'd missed most of my prom, so I asked him to take me home.

> *aww he was so considerate of my needs!*

The reality was, I couldn't speak up for myself and allowed him to treat me that way. So afraid of losing him, I thought I needed to do everything he wanted me to do. We didn't have a normal relationship. He was gorgeous and I convinced myself I loved him, but we didn't connect in any way. We weren't best friends who talked to each other, he never asked about my life and what I wanted to do with it and I didn't ask about his. He just talked about all the money he was going to make and I'd listen, thinking how much more important his life sounded compared to mine.

About a year after our first date, he began pulling back and I began to panic and cling to him.

noooo. please no

The more he pulled back, the more desperate and needy I became until one day he broke up with me. It happened on a Sunday morning while we were working together in another of his family's businesses, the local video shop. Just before we shut shop for the afternoon, he called me into the back room and told me he was too busy for a girlfriend and wanted us to be friends.

what does that mean, 'too busy for a girlfriend'?
who the fuck says that!!

He said he loved me, but was just too busy and of course, I asked him not to finish it.

actually it was more like begged him

Realising I wasn't giving up that easily, he went straight for the jugular and gave it to me straight. "I don't want to be with you anymore," he said and my world stopped. I went home, tail between my legs and cried for days. When my tears dried up, I wondered what I'd do with my time now.

I didn't grieve for him, the boy I supposedly loved so much. I grieved for me and how I was going to fill my time without him. Eventually,

about two weeks later

I pulled myself together and decided I wanted him back. Having discussed it with Claire, we both agreed that the best way to do that was to date someone else. I knew a boy who was interested, so I called him and asked him out. We had a lovely date but my heart wasn't in it, so I asked him to drop me home with the intention of finishing it before it started. Parked outside my house, I kissed him goodnight but as I did so, my ex-boyfriend drove by and I was thrilled.

Plan revised, I arranged another date

Each time I made sure to kiss him outside my house

the poor guy really liked me
but I was on a mission

and within two weeks it worked like a charm.

My ex turned up at my front door and I leapt into his arms feeling like I'd won, but of course I hadn't. I didn't hold back or become unavailable to him, I didn't make him work for me, instead I offered my soul on a plate and he took it. I forgot about my own life again and being with him was all that mattered. We were never truly back together. We weren't boyfriend and girlfriend, it was all on his terms and that meant sex whenever he had a spare five minutes. Again I convinced myself it was enough, I told myself, I loved him and I'd take him anyway I could get him.

I wish I'd told him to piss off
I wish I'd had the strength to walk away,
because in my heart I knew he was using me;
but I was seventeen,
in love and unable to stop myself.

Each time he came to my house or took me out in his car, usually to the Pope's cross in the Phoenix Park to have sex, I was convinced he'd ask me to be his girlfriend again, but he never did. I was always waiting.

In the two years since we'd officially broken up,

but still having sex

I'd never been on a single date with him. He just used me for sex and I let him. After my exams, I decided to become a gym instructor and got a part time job at a very exclusive health club on the outskirts of Dublin. I was delighted, because my 'non boyfriend' was also a member and this was another way for me to be around him.

Thankfully though and within a few short months, I gained a new perspective. No longer the silly schoolgirl, I was working, earning money, enjoying my life and for the first time in years realised there were other men in the world; men who were far more interesting and really interested in me, men who wanted to take me out on dates and have some fun. Finally realising my worth,

temporarily

I walked away and it was as if the last three years had never happened. I never looked back.

Working at the gym meant I was a gym bunny during the day, but I was definitely a party girl at night. My sister Audrey was my best friend and with a couple of other girlfriends we were considered the Annabel's girls.

The hottest nightspot in Dublin
where we went most Friday,
Saturday and Sunday nights.

When the club finished at two am, it was straight down to Leeson Street to party until five am where someone usually bought us cheap champagne

if we were pissed enough to snog them for it

and if they didn't, we drank water. Partying was life and I loved it.

18 months after I started working at the gym, I got a letter,

no email in those days

from a couple of school friends who'd moved to London. They were living in Camden Town and asked if I wanted to join them. I'd thought about living abroad, but always thought it would be America. London had never crossed my mind, but the idea grew on me and a week later I handed in my notice at work, booked a flight to Heathrow and moved to London.

I've never needed long to make decisions,
still don't.

It was a rainy Friday night in November 1992, I stood with my mother, two sisters and my Aunty Carmel at the departure gates of Dublin airport. My older sister cried as she was going to miss her party girl, my younger sister was only seven years old and didn't really know what was going on. My mother was quiet and a bit teary and my Aunty Carmel told me to have a ball. I was quite upbeat. I thought London would be great for a while, but I didn't believe for a second it would work out and planned to be home by Christmas.

4: London Baby

There's nowhere else like London. Nothing at all, anywhere.
 - ***Vivienne Westwood***

Just like that, I was living in London. It was amazing, exciting and terrifying all combined together and I loved it.

Fascinated by the busyness of Heathrow, I took my first tube ride to Camden Town where I initially lived with my friend Catherine, at her sister's flat. We eventually saved enough money for our own place and an amazing warehouse apartment at Tower Hill became our first real home in London.

Sharing with two other girls, we lived in a great location overlooking the Thames but the rent was so high, we never had any money. A little thing like that however didn't stop us going out to bars and clubs nearly every night and life became one big party. Getting into the best clubs and restaurants in London was our only goal and when our neighbours turned out to be four guys who worked in the city, we were thrilled.

jackpot! they had loads of parties and booze at their flat

I dated the American one and although I wasn't really into him, that didn't stop me going out with him. He said he wanted to show me his London lifestyle, the restaurants, the parties and the champagne, so I let him.

atta girl Suzanne, as superficial as you can get
classy

Needless to say it didn't last long; did he break it off or did I? I can't remember, but I continued partying my way through

32

London without him and basically having a ball. I did go to work, but that didn't inspire me in the slightest; life was all about going out and drinking as much free champagne as I could get my hands on. Before I knew it, a year had flown by and the symptoms began: constant headaches, dizziness and blurred vision.

all of which I completely ignored for as long as possible.

I knew what was going on, and when they persisted, I had no choice but to go and see a doctor and because of my medical history, was immediately referred to a specialist in London, sent for an MRI scan and a week later the bad news was delivered. The brain tumour I had when I was 16 had returned to bite me in the ass. I was gutted.

I say it returned, it had never really gone

It was being reduced by medication that I was supposed to take daily, however I'd stopped taking the medication shortly after I moved to London, for what I considered to be two very good reasons: (1) the symptoms were gone and believing I knew more than all the doctors who had treated me over the years, I decided that meant the brain tumour was gone;

Dr Suzanne Selvester MD

(2) living in London meant I was usually hungover to hell, the medication and alcohol combo made me feel worse, so one of them had to go.

It wasn't going to be alcohol.

33

It sounds crazy as I write it, but I wanted to fit in with my friends and not be the sick one. I'd used this illness when I was seventeen for bunking off school and it suited me then, but now it was interrupting my life. I was having fun and didn't want to be throwing up every morning from the amount of Bromocriptine and alcohol in my body. It was so unfair, I told myself as I wallowed in self-pity. The fact that I was seriously ill didn't even cross my mind.

rock and roll Suzanne.

When the endocrinologist at The Royal London Hospital saw my MRI results, he was shocked at my lack of responsibility and I was mortified. He knew I'd stopped taking the medication and quite simply couldn't understand why. To be honest I didn't blame him for being pissed off at me. I was completely in the wrong and my tumour had now doubled in size, was leaning against the glands of my eyes. I was in danger of losing my eyesight. Like a kick in the teeth, I was forced to face up to the whole thing and felt so hard done by. Immediate surgery followed and all the years of taking medication to prevent it were wasted.

After the surgery, I spent two weeks at the Royal London Hospital in Whitechapel and then needed two months off for convalescence, so I went home to Dublin.

wings were well and truly clipped

Grounded due to the effects of cabin pressure on my newly fixed brain, my sister flew to London and we began a long and arduous drive to Holyhead, to take the ferry home. As we sailed into Dublin Port, I was still vomiting into the toilet, wondering if the air pressure might have been a better option than three hours of seasickness, but I was home and that's all that mattered.

When my ex non-boyfriend,

the one I'd loved and dreamed about marrying since I was 15,

turned up and asked me to be his girlfriend, I almost laughed. How ironic that he now offered me everything I'd ever wanted, but it was too late. He'd dominated my teenage years but now I simply wasn't interested. I needed to heal, but I was also impatient to get back to my life. Even though I had to take 17 steroid tablets a day which made me feel awful, I recovered quickly.

My mother wouldn't let me do anything for myself,

swoon

she waited on me hand and foot. It was lovely, but very soon I was going stir crazy and wanted to get out of there. I wasn't staying in Dublin, I absolutely knew that, but I was unsure if I wanted to go back to London.

hmmmmmm... what to do?

One morning I opened an Irish newspaper and read a headline that said: *American Embassy offering green cards to Irish citizens.* Well of course it was a direct message from the Universe, so I applied, got one. That was it, I was going to America. It's what I always wanted to do. I was going to move there and live the life of my dreams. Feeling excited about my decision, I first had to go back to London, where my job was

35

being held and tie things up. I also had to somehow save enough money for the big move.

even on my minimum wage income and
extortionate outgoings? I was optimistic.

Having spent nearly 10 weeks recovering in Dublin, being back in the big smoke felt great and I soon fell back into the flow of my life again. I was working in a shop in Covent Garden, but my New York dream was never far from my mind. I was desperate to get there. I figured if I saved a fiver every week, I'd get there when I was about 60.

still optimistic

One night while out drinking cocktails with the girls from work, an absolutely unbelievable coincidence occurred. Halfway through my third Long Island Iced Tea, a guy at the bar started talking to me. He was English but worked in America as a stockbroker and thought I'd make a great trainee apprentice for a new desk he was setting up in London. Of course, I totally agreed with him and tried to sound casual,

almost choking on my drink

as I told him so. I realised a total stranger was offering me a job, with a company whose base was in New York! He called his boss right there and then and arranged for me to have lunch with him the following week and I couldn't actually believe what was happening. I wanted it so badly, so by the time I eventually met Jack at a restaurant in Covent Garden, I was a nervous wreck but I didn't need to worry. As soon as he heard my Irish accent,

he was third generation Irish

we immediately connected and I landed the job. I was now the trainee Forward Yen Broker for Cantor Fitzgerald. My salary doubled overnight and my training was taking place in, wait for it... New York City.

Ta daaaaa.

I'd gone back to London with the intention of raising the money to fulfill my childhood dream of going to America. Now I had a green card, a job sending me to New York and the realisation that I was the luckiest girl on the planet.

the Universe obviously singled me out,
I always knew I was special.

A month later I arrived in New York City and it felt like I'd come home. I lived in Hoboken and worked on the 104th floor of the World Trade Centre. Everything about America resonated with me. I floated through the streets of Manhattan in complete awe. The smells, the traffic, the people - I loved it all. During the day, I learned how to be a money broker and at night I went out with the boys from work drinking in all the cool Manhattan bars.

I wanted to stay and live there forever and hoped against hope the company would let me, but a few short weeks later, they sent me back to the new desk in London and I was gutted.

Looking back I often think I should have stayed. I could have gotten a different job, even if it was in a bar. I had a green card, I had friends who would let me crash on their sofas, but I didn't listen to my instinct

instinct! what's that?

and was afraid to ask for what I wanted. I avoided the discomfort of speaking up for myself and missed out on a lot of opportunities in my life. On this occasion I cried all the way back to London as my New York dream melted away. However, working with thousands of male stockbrokers in London everyday wasn't hard

someone's gotta do it, right?

and I soon settled into my life. I had a great new flat, a cool new flatmate and I had money. I was still taking steroids following my surgery, but they didn't affect me like the pre-surgery medication. Everything was getting back to normal. I missed being in New York and wanted to get back there, but my life in London was good and I felt happy. Of course it was then that my world was turned upside down.

To my absolute and utter disbelief, I got pregnant. Having been told by my doctors when diagnosed with my tumour that I was infertile, this was a big fucking surprise. Always careful against STDs, I never

well not often

had sex without a condom, but here I was looking at two blue lines on a pregnancy test wondering what the hell I was going to do now. I was nowhere near ready to be a mother and sobbed in the arms of my flatmate. We talked about it and thinking long and hard, I decided to have an abortion. The doctor told me the steroids I was taking could offer a huge risk to the foetus, but it was little comfort. I don't like to dwell on this part of the story. It was a very difficult time in my life and when the procedure was completed, I drowned in grief.

but only briefly

I checked into the clinic alone on a Sunday afternoon and checked out alone on Tuesday morning. I took the tube home, climbed into bed and cried for two days. On the third day I went back to work. I pushed everything to the back of my mind, didn't process any of my grief. I just threw myself back into my job and my partying ways.

A sensible and healthy approach to processing grief!

Three days was all I gave myself, then I blocked out the excruciating feelings of guilt and remorse that were trying to tear me apart. A couple of months later the lease on my flat came to an end, my flatmate moved in with her boyfriend and I found myself living in Notting Hill Gate with a girl I'd never met before. She was lovely and our flat was in the attic of an old Victorian town house. It had a fantastic roof terrace where we'd sit on Saturday afternoons, drinking wine and smoking cigarettes while looking over the rooftops of West London. My neighbour was the famous actress Julie Christie,

I only mixed with the best

who I'd often talk to while waiting for my clothes to dry.

The dryer was in the hall outside her apartment.

My life was back on track, I had my job, another cool apartment and of course my great friends, but there were times when I felt so overwhelmed by loneliness that it stopped me in my tracks. I'd go to work, come home, eat and go to bed, then do the same

39

thing the next day. On weekends I usually got pissed with my flatmate,

or on my own

because most of my friends were now in relationships and I was sick of feeling like a third wheel. When my boss called me into his office a few weeks before Christmas to tell me he didn't think I was up to the pressure of being a broker, I agreed with him. It was a relief and he was right, the only thing I liked about the job was flirting with the guys in the office and the free drinks after work.

a very nice perk

I worked a couple of weeks notice, told my landlord I was leaving, packed up my stuff and moved back to Dublin...again.

Another year had passed and I was once again going home. This time my ex non-boyfriend

yes, still the same one from when I was fifteen.

drove to London and brought me and two years of my life home and once again I was back in Dublin, with no clue as to what was next. My ex still wanted me back but that ship had definitely sailed and I had no interest. A few weeks later I was sitting in my mother's kitchen, drinking tea, watching the rain and reflecting on my life and once again made the decision to move to America. I loved my time in London, but I really wanted to go back to New York. I still had my green card, I knew people there. I'd work in Dublin for a couple of months and earn some money,

no massive outgoings and the rent at home was free

then pick up my dream and move back to America. I was going with what felt right, but as it transpired, the Universe had something else in mind.

5: A Crossroads in My Life

I Stood at a Crossroads and Fate Came To Meet Me.
  - *Liz Greene*

It was January 1995 when my life plan changed again. I was working in Dublin, saving money for my big move and really enjoying being home.

except for the weather

Ireland was in the grips of one of the coldest winters we'd seen in years and it was miserable. One Saturday afternoon I was in a pub with my sister and friends watching rugby. Ireland were playing England at Lansdowne Road. England eventually smashed us by 20 points to eight so we continued to drown our sorrows by drinking and singing songs.

Irish style

As the evening wore on we found ourselves back in our old haunt, Annabel's nightclub, which was packed with lovely English rugby fans. Exciting for us as it was something new. Following a night of dancing, drinking and flirting, I was outside the club waiting for a taxi, freezing my ass off in a short skirt and snogging the face off some random guy when I noticed my sister walking by with a rather attractive looking man. Without a second thought for the guy I was kissing,

you're going home alone bud!

I ran after them to share a taxi home. We walked down Leeson Street desperate to find a taxi, but it seemed as if every person in Dublin was doing the same thing, so we just kept walking.

The man was English and thought he'd hit the jackpot with a sister on each arm.

he was definitely enjoying the Irish hospitality

He was visiting Dublin for the first time on a rugby tour, had separated from his group and was trying to make his way back to Bray, a town a few miles outside of Dublin. As we walked and talked, I found I liked him very much and out of the blue asked if he'd like to kiss me.

what? snogging two men in one night?
I considered that a positive.

'Would you like to kiss me?' I asked out of nowhere and he didn't hesitate when he said yes. It was then that I experienced my first ever out of body kiss from a man. 4am on a freezing cold night, in the middle of Grafton Street Kevin kissed me for the first time and the world literally stopped. My sister simply rolled her eyes, not caring one bit as she already had a boyfriend.

I'd never been kissed like that before, it was the kiss to end all kisses, and as we stood there wrapped around each other, the world started spinning again. Pulling apart, we both started laughing, shocked at the connection we felt and saying, 'holy shit' at the same time.

chemistry

Soon afterwards we found a couple of taxis and agreed to meet the following night at Annabel's. When I woke the next morning, it took some time for me to realise I'd met a man who'd literally swept me off my feet. I couldn't believe it and didn't know it was possible to feel so connected to someone I'd just met; but I felt it and was positive he felt it too. Deep in my heart, I knew this man would be significant in my life.

deep in my heart, I wanted him to be.

When I met him in Annabel's the following night, I flew into his arms and spent the night stuck to him. We danced, talked, kissed and got to know each other, oblivious to everyone else in the club. Suddenly I had a dilemma. A mere 24 hours earlier my life path had been sorted. I was going to America to live my dream, but now I wasn't sure if I should go back to London instead and explore this connection with Kevin.

fuck. plan B?

Now, as fate would have it, a couple of days later the decision was seemingly taken out of my hands when my green card disappeared into thin air. I'd left it on top of the mantelpiece in my mother's lounge and could only assume it had somehow slipped down the back and into the fire. Perhaps I could have gone to the American Embassy to get another one, but I took it as a sign from the Universe and booked a flight back to London.

America was too far away anyway!
who wants to live there?

London was easy and getting a job was easier. I made some phone calls, secured one with my old company and a week later, I was back living in London...again. 'Third time lucky' I thought as I walked through Stansted airport. With no place of my own, I slept on a friend's sofa and within a week of being back, had my first date with Kevin: a drink at a Covent Garden pub, *Interview with A Vampire* at the Odeon Leicester Square and later, the first orgasm I'd ever received from a man.

44

OH! the guy is supposed to do that to your body!!

I was 23 years old and couldn't believe what I'd been missing. Faking it for years, I honestly thought there was something wrong with me. To finally meet someone who knew how to turn me on felt like I'd died and gone to heaven.

orgasmic heaven

An immediate relationship developed. I'd work during the week and stay at my friend's house. Then on Friday nights get the train to Kevin's house in West London where he'd pick me up from the station and take me to dinner. We'd then spend the weekend either meeting up with friends, going to the rugby club or staying in bed.

more orgasms, I had a lot of catching up to do!

On Monday morning, he'd drop me back to the train station and off I'd go to work again.

After a few weeks of to-ing and fro-ing, I decided to get my own place and began looking for a room to rent. When Kevin offered for me to stay with him until I found one, I jumped at the chance. Nine months later, when I was still there and he officially asked me to move in, I of course said yes and dragged him to Ikea.

a girl can't be expected to live
without rugs, cushions and girly things

He was happy to let me make the changes. We were very much in love and I loved being part of a couple. When I took him to Dublin to meet my family for the first time, he made the mistake

45

of trying to keep up with my dad, drinking pint for pint. Needless to say they both fell out of the pub together, a perfect initiation in my family and he was welcomed with open arms. A couple of years later, we bought our first home together and soon after that, Kevin asked me to marry him. I immediately said yes. My life was complete. I had a great man, a good job, a gorgeous little house and on top of all that, a fabulous wedding to plan. I was happy.

right?

I ignored the feeling that something wasn't quite right. I had everything, but the feeling of jubilation I thought would accompany a marriage proposal just wasn't there. I thought I'd feel more; I wanted to feel more. Of course as I'd done many times over the years, I convinced myself I was happy and dampened my doubts by getting busy. I distracted myself by focusing on our perfect home, our perfect wedding and of course our perfect life.

Distract, distract, distract
and miss your life sailing by

At the time, I was unaware of what self-sabotage was. I didn't know the happiness I sought so badly was an inside job and always found ways to doubt myself. I became irrationally insecure within a few months of being engaged. Nothing had changed, we were in love, everything was great but... I felt unworthy of it and convinced myself Kevin was going to be unfaithful. At times it felt as if I wanted him to, just to prove myself right

seriously fucked up perception

and when he wasn't looking, I'd check his emails and phone messages for proof. My anxiety soaring through the roof. I'd tell myself I needed to know if the hordes of women I imagined throwing themselves at him on a daily basis were real.

He was a businessman and a rugby player. He was often out with clients or away on rugby tours and my insecurity elevated to the point of feeling physically sick at the thought of his infidelity. This was further aggravated by his flirty nature and his teasing of me; he liked to keep me guessing which was more damaging than he ever knew.

I knew I was being ridiculous,

but I couldn't let it go.

I believed I had no right to this

why did he want to be with me again?

and compared myself to everyone I met. I'd wonder why he didn't want all the gorgeous babes who obviously wanted him. Women who probably had a more successful career than me,

I was obviously as thick as two planks

they could contribute to the finances, rather than being bailed out of credit card debt.

I was such a loser

Women who came from better families, because even though I loved my family, at that time I felt ashamed of our working class status. I thought everyone was better than me and my self-esteem hit rock bottom. A local therapist helped me get a handle on it and together we discovered unresolved grief

no surprise there

and feelings of not being good enough, probably from my teenage years when I'd allowed my first boyfriend to use me for sex.

no shit Sherlock

Now that I was in a proper relationship, I was waiting for the bubble to burst, because that's what normally happened, right? It took a few months of talking it through for me to gain a different perspective and release some of the destructive thoughts I had. Kevin was encouraging, he'd tell me he loved me and didn't understand why I put myself through so much crap. Of course, I'd immediately question the motive behind such a comment.

was he trying to throw me off the scent?

The poor guy couldn't win, but his view on life was more simple than mine. He loved me, he loved his job and he lived his life the best way he could. I, on the other hand, was a complete over-thinker who analysed everything. On top of that, I was an emotional mess who drove him and myself crazy.

complicated anyone?

My state of mind improved; slightly, not completely, but I told Kevin it was all sorted and the look of relief on his face told me I'd done the right thing. He never knew the extent of my self-sabotage, because neither did I. I was completely unaware of how much I glossed over my problems and suppressed them. Not being honest with him was a mistake and a pattern of behaviour in our relationship was formed that would continue throughout.

I could never speak my truth to him

I didn't value myself enough to think he'd stick around if I was anything less than perfect. I felt under enormous pressure to look good and in my mind that meant to look skinny, so I was always on a diet. The voice in my head would tell me that my fiancé needed to be with a popular, attractive, skinny girl and come hell or high water that was going to be me. The fact that he might just love me for who I was never entered my mind.

don't be stupid Suzanne, love you for you? ridiculous

Equally as guilty, physical appearance meant everything to Kevin and if I did gain a few pounds, which of course as a yo-yo dieter I did, he'd make small comments about it which would crucify me.

Things did get better though. I got a new job, we were busy planning the wedding and I confronted some of my insecurities. If negative thoughts attacked, I was better at letting them go and my life fell into a nice flow. We had a routine. On weekdays we both went to work and on weekends we fixed up our new house, bought furniture, painted walls and so on. Before we knew it, three and a half years passed and the time had come to walk down the aisle and marry the man I loved.

6: Love & Marriage

If I get married, I want to be very married.
-   ***Audrey Hepburn***

My wedding day was the grandest of grand affairs in Dublin with over two hundred friends and family flying in from all over the world. I worked relentlessly to make sure glamorous and romantic was the theme and as the first person in my immediate family to get married, we were all bursting with excitement. The night before the wedding we hosted a pre wedding dinner at a restaurant in Temple Bar and as the wine and conversation flowed, everyone got to know each other before the main event.

Then on Saturday, June 13th 1998 at The University Church on St Stephen's Green, I married Kevin. Having decided when I was nine years old that I'd get married in this church, I finally did.

my life was complete and
my search for happiness was over

Following a beautiful ceremony, my new husband and I crossed the road, followed by our guests and walked through St Stephen's Green, a park in central Dublin to the Shelborne Hotel on the other side. It could not have been more perfect.

even though it was pissing down rain

We had our photographs taken in the rain, but we didn't care one bit. The atmosphere was almost carnival as two hundred guests walked and laughed in the lashing rain, most carrying broken umbrellas. Nothing could dampen our spirits.

I felt so happy watching my family and friends as they celebrated with us and put the familiar niggling in my stomach down to wedding day nerves. I loved my new husband. We were a great couple and I had my happy ending.

so piss off voice in my head

Anything else was pushed far from my mind and I enjoyed every second of my wedding day and then our honeymoon touring Singapore, Hong Kong and Thailand. I felt like the luckiest girl in the world; I had a husband, I had a home and I had a plan for our future together.

If I'd had any self-awareness, I might have recognised my feelings of discontent, something deep within me telling me to pay attention to my own dreams and stop with the checklist lifestyle. Stop distracting myself from who I was and what I wanted from my life. My own ambitions were pushed aside in favour of my husband's happiness and success.

not by him, by me.

I made his needs more relevant than mine, his ambition more of a priority and his success more important. While that might work for some couples, it didn't for me and deep down I knew it. I wanted more from my life, but ignored the feeling that I was overlooking something and began planning our future based on his success. Making the plans, thinking ahead, arranging, orchestrating and generally mapping out our future.

It was absolutely his responsibility to make it all happen and to make me deliriously happy

I didn't look too closely at what I wasn't doing to make myself happy, to make my own dreams come true

that was his job

and on the rare occasion when I did stop, my soul screamed at me that something was wrong. My life lacked depth and meaning, but of course I'd ignore it by planning even more.

I was 26 years old and settling into married life. Kevin and I had already been living together for three years, so the only difference was that we wore wedding rings. We went to work, met at home in the evening for dinner. Weekends were spent with friends or decorating the house and my fear of living a conventional life with routine was long forgotten and exactly how it had turned out.

A year later I was pregnant and never super excited about my job, this was another excuse to relinquish responsibility for my professional life, so I gave up my job at three months pregnant. I told myself and my husband I needed to rest and prepare for the baby and spent my days reading, relaxing, decorating the nursery and living for the day when my baby was due, 1st of January 2000. Sean however arrived two weeks early and was born on December 17th, 1999. A fabulous early Christmas present.

There were no words to describe how I felt becoming a mother for the first time. Overwhelmed with love for my son, this little boy was everything as I was overcome with an indescribable sense of protectiveness toward him. It was me and him against the world and I didn't even want my family or friends holding him when they came to visit.

Having him enabled my heart to burst open and I was overwhelmed by the love I felt for him. I know most mothers feel this and it's beautiful, but for me it was my first experience of true love and as I looked at my beautiful baby boy, I was besieged by emotions I'd never felt before. He was an angel who slept most of the time, hardly ever cried and was the perfect baby. I felt so blessed to have such a gorgeous son. Kevin was also completely smitten and spent every possible minute with him, hurrying home from work so he could bathe and hold him as he slept. We would both spend hours just gazing at Sean, both so much in love with him. Very soon however something completely unexpected happened that smashed our world to bits.

It was Monday morning and I was in bed snoozing. Sean was fed, changed and laying happily in his crib when I woke to the sound of heavy footsteps on the stairs and almost had a heart attack.

who the fuck is that?

The bedroom door opened and Kevin walked in carrying a cardboard box and instinctively I knew something was wrong. He put the box of personal things from his desk onto the bed, picked up his son and told me he'd been fired. Having already resigned from my own job, I couldn't breathe as I spiraled into panic. My insecurity with money immediately triggered and I was back sitting on the stairs as a child,

washing machine stomach activated

53

listening to my mother crying and worrying about paying the bills. Kevin tried to reassure me, but I was in full doomsday mode. We were spenders, we enjoyed ourselves and saving for a rainy day was the last thing on our minds. Suddenly we had a very rainy day with not a penny saved, a mortgage to pay and a new baby to feed.

> *oh my god he was going to starve,*
> *we'd starve, we'd have to live on the streets,*
> *in a tent, Sean would be put in care.*

Kevin immediately reached out to colleagues in his industry and arranged meetings for the following week. The house was valued because not only had he been fired, he was also being sued. The equity in the house would be needed to pay it off and I was heartbroken at the thought of Sean not spending any time in his beautiful nursery. I tried not to blame Kevin, I really did but having no concept of personal responsibility, that's all I could do. I knew it was unfair, but blaming him was all I knew how to do.

> *what the fuck?*
> *How could you let this happen?*

I was postpartum, irrational, tired, scared and losing my home, the first security I'd ever known.

With plans already in place to go to Dublin and introduce Sean to my family, we went two days after the firing. I did my best to put on a positive show, not easy under the circumstances. My life had been turned upside down and I was struggling to cope, but I pulled myself together.

> *barely*

54

On the Friday night while at my mother's house, I began feeling unwell. My asthma flared, I knew the symptoms so didn't think too much about it and took my inhaler. The next morning, I still felt bad and considered a visit to the doctor, but we were going shopping so I decided it could wait until later and ignored my shortness of breath.

who needs breath when you have money to spend ?
oh wait, we haven't got that anymore.

Kevin went to the pub with my dad to watch rugby and I took my mother and my sisters into town, then to visit my Aunty Carmel with Sean. We were walking around Brown Thomas Store in Dublin and I could barely take two steps without being out of breath. My sister and my mother glanced nervously at each other, but I shushed them, telling them I was fine. I didn't have time for this. We needed to get my mother something to wear for my brother's wedding and having an asthma attack wasn't part of the plan. However, when we left town to drive to my aunt's house, I spotted a sign for Beaumont Hospital and took a left turn and headed towards it.

last minute instinctive decision

By the time I parked the car, I couldn't breathe at all and almost crawled into the hospital reception where complete chaos ensued as I fainted.

mid conversation with the emergency room receptionist.

The lack of oxygen in my blood was critical, I was picked up off the floor and immediately rushed to a side room where the doctors and nurses tried to help me. When I came round, I was on a nebuliser, had an intravenous cannula to get steroids into me as fast as possible, Sean was screaming to be fed and my mother and sister had turned the colour of a sheet.

a nice shade of pasty grey.

About 20 minutes later, everything calmed down, I could breathe again with the help of oxygen and the steroids. My mother, sister and baby were all by my side but Sean was screaming blue murder. He was hungry and wanted to be fed, but I could no longer feed him. My milk was now contaminated by the steroids in my bloodstream, so my sister took my car and drove home, via a supermarket for bottles, a steriliser and baby formula. When they left, I lay there trying very hard to relax and ignore the panic I felt at being separated from my son.

A couple of hours later, Kevin and my mother arrived back at the hospital and we waited together for me to be discharged. I still felt unwell, but I remembered the drill: a couple of goes on a nebuliser, a course of steroids and then home, that's what usually happened.

but not this time

Quite out of the blue and while talking to my husband, I couldn't breathe again

as in, not at all

My airways closed completely and I felt as if I was suffocating. I'd never felt anything like it before, as if someone had their hand over my mouth and nose, I couldn't take a breath. Kevin ran for the nurse and once again chaos ensued as I passed out for the second time that day.

My last memory was of a doctor in a white coat running towards my bed with a syringe in his hand. When I woke up I was on a ward with my husband and mother beside my bed. The doctor explained the level of oxygen in my bloodstream was so critically low, had I been anywhere other than the hospital when the second attack occurred, I would have died.

holy shit!

That last minute decision to take a left turn to the hospital had saved my life and I felt like someone was looking out for me. I had to stay in hospital for four days

four days!

and I was devastated at being away from my son. Kevin brought him to visit, but I felt like our bonding was interrupted, because I could no longer breastfeed him.

When I was released, we flew back to the UK the same evening. Kevin received a phone call from an old work associate who wanted to meet ASAP and I insisted we go. That very next afternoon, along with two business partners, Kevin set up a new engineering company and with contracts already in place, they could receive immediate salaries - and I could breathe again.

literally

The stress of Kevin losing his job had caused my asthma attack and although I knew my fear of poverty was irrational, it was powerful enough to nearly kill me. As I recovered from the trauma, I no longer cared that we had to sell our house,

57

it had to happen and I was alive. It took 18 months to finalise the sale and we then moved from Surrey to Essex to be near my childhood friend Catherine, who by then had two girls and I wanted our kids to grow up together.

Kevin worked for what seemed like 24 hours a day over the next couple of years and I stayed home with Sean. I fell into a routine, doing all the things a new mother does: baby group meetings, kiddie play dates, trips to the park. Most of the time I felt content with my life.

When Sean was two years old, Kevin and I went through a difficult patch in our marriage. We no longer seemed connected and I was unsure if we'd make it, but we talked and decided we still wanted to be married.

Soon after that our second son was born and our peace was shattered. Ethan kicked and screamed his way into the world, completely destroying my illusion that motherhood was easy. He cried day and night, nothing would stop him.

He was also the most beautiful little boy with blond hair, green eyes and olive skin. I adored him and so did everyone else. People would stop in the street just to look at him. Sean however was less impressed and would often ask why his baby brother cried so much. I didn't really know, so I'd simply answer, "Because he just likes being heard."

Two short years after that, Sammie arrived

swoon

and I was once again smitten. Sammie was an absolute angel, easy going and sleepy. He just wanted to eat and sleep. Nothing seemed to bother him, which was a godsend because by now Ethan was in the terrible two phase and very challenging. I had three beautiful sons, a successful husband and a gorgeous home. Kevin's business went from strength to strength which meant our lifestyle had improved dramatically.

we were on the up!

We'd bought a new house which we extensively renovated, had regular five-star holidays, wonderful weekends away with friends, money in the bank and private school for Sean. I'd nailed it. I was living the dream. Now and then I'd feel like something was missing, but would reprimand myself for being stupid and selfish.

does complete happiness exist for anyone?
get over yourself Suzanne

The years soon flew by. We moved again to an even bigger house

definitely on the up

that overlooked the countryside, the children were all at school, my husband was running an empire and I could do or have anything I wanted. Maria, my Portuguese housekeeper helped me with the house.

another angel

She cooked and cleaned and took care of the children so shopping trips to London, spa days with the girls or long boozy lunches were the norm. I was living my champagne lifestyle and Selfridges was my favourite place to be. My biggest complaint was the amount of packing and unpacking I had to do.

due to the amount of the holidays we went on

So deeply entangled in my illusion, I was caught up in my materialist existence and I didn't even know it.

how am I supposed to unpack from February half term skiing in Switzerland, then shop and repack in time for America, Dubai or Australia at Easter? such an unreasonable expectation

The illusion kept me distracted and able to ignore the part of me that dreamed of having a career, of being my own person and doing something with my own life. I'd think about the things I wanted to do,

be a TV presenter and write a book

but it seemed like an impossible dream, because it was too hard

no one makes it in the world of TV and writing

and anyway, I was terrified of failure and even more terrified of what people would think. Imagine the ridicule I'd be subjected to if I dared confess my ambitions.

lol, get her!

Deep down I knew I wanted to find my purpose. I wanted something more than motherhood, because although I loved my children, I felt unfulfilled. I wanted to do something with my life, to make an impact on the world, but I completely lacked belief in myself to do so and felt so unworthy of it.

bummer

As time went on, my relationship with Kevin became somewhat dysfunctional and my self-esteem plummeted even further. I knew Kevin loved me, but I felt lonely and there was distance between us. He'd come home from work in the evenings, we'd get the kids to bed, then watch TV in the lounge while eating dinner. The conversation became less and it seemed we only talked about the children, or how much money we made, what holiday we were going on next, what else we could do to extend the house or let's buy a new one.

a bigger one

Living completely in the future, everything we wanted was always one step away and never right now. I'd often watch other couples with envy, longing for the intimacy and friendship I perceived them to have. Kevin and I no longer had it and I missed it. I felt like he didn't know me, he only saw a superficial version of me

because that's all I was capable of showing him or anyone.

and over time our relationship felt like hard work. Somehow we'd both managed to convince ourselves that everything was ok, but now and then Kevin would say, "You don't love me anymore, do you?"

no I don't, but I really, really want to

61

I'd laugh at him and say of course I do. I knew there was something wrong, but I never imagined anything else in my life. As far as I was concerned we were married, we were a family and we were staying that way.

7: An Epiphany

The secret of a happy marriage, remains a secret.
-    ***Henry Youngman***

In the blink of an eye we were ten years married, it was October half term and we were on holiday in Dubai, somewhere we went every year with the children. Forty degrees at 11am was just fine because I was lying on a lounger, at The Le Meridian Hotel on Jumeriah Beach. White sandy beaches, staff that fell over themselves to serve you and a kids club to die for. The boys now eight, five and three were playing in the pool with their dad and as usual I was stretched out, tanning myself and wondering if it was too early to have a cocktail.

Pina Colada or Long island iced tea?
decisions, decisions

Flicking through my magazine, I gazed lovingly at the massive diamond rock on my finger. A gift for our tenth wedding anniversary

four carats

and I was completely in love with it. Giving my attention to the other guests in the hotel as they took their positions around the pool, I found it funny that we all went to the same spot everyday. These were our sunbeds for at least 10 days and my husband paid the towels clerk for the privilege.

The hotel was full of beautiful people, the women glamorous and the men handsome. As usual I felt fat and frumpy and although not fat at all, I had so much self-loathing, that even being a size zero wouldn't have made me happy.

You are disgusting, how can you let yourself go like this!

I could only see my flaws and constantly compared myself

very unfavourably

to everyone else. I hated my body and wondered how I even left the room in a bikini. As I continued my browse of the other guests, a random but crystal clear thought entered my head, 'What are these people doing to make themselves happy, that I just can't seem to figure out?'

Still living with the notion that everyone was better than me, I thought they had it all. They looked happier than me, their family life was probably better, they probably had a nicer house and their kids probably went to a better school.

the bottomless pit of wanting more

The women were slimmer and their husbands probably earned more than mine, therefore we had no right to be there and wouldn't belong in a million years. Just your average holiday thoughts running through my head as I lay there looking as cool as a cucumber, in the lap of luxury.

My husband throwing the kids around the pool caught my attention and as I watched them I thought about it again, 'What is everyone else doing to make themselves happy, that I just can't seem to figure out?'

fuck, am I not happy?

64

It's hard to describe exactly what happened next, but suddenly I couldn't breathe as an epiphany hit me square between my eyes. 'Oh my god, I'm not happy, I'm sad and lonely and just pretending everything is great.' In a state of blind panic, I left the pool and ran towards our room. Pacing like a tiger as I waited for the lift, I tried to figure out what had just happened and when I got to our room, I went straight to the bathroom, leaned over the toilet and threw up. I wasn't sad and lonely, I was happy damn it. My kids were happy, my husband was happy, I was living the life of my dreams and everything was great so WTF?

Trying to calm myself down, I began a checklist in my head, to convince myself that everything was ok.

I had the life I always wanted, *Check.*

I had a dependable and ambitious husband who was a fantastic dad and a great provider, *Check.*

I had a big house, a nice car, lots of holidays and the kids all went to private school, *check, check, check.*

Everything was ok, everything had come together and I had the life of my dreams, so what was the problem?

eh?....

Suddenly the feeling that something was missing, a feeling I'd pushed away for years forced its way to the forefront of my mind and it asked one question. What about love?

fuck

What about love Suzanne? I didn't want to answer, I didn't want to admit that might be the root of my discontent, the cause of my unhappiness, but I knew I could no longer avoid it.

Was I in love with my husband?

65

Not really

Had I ever been in love with him?

> *yes, in a dysfunctional and co-dependent way*

Was I even capable of real love?

> *not yet, but you will be in the future*

Did I need love to be happy?

> *yes, but you need self-love first*

I felt so confused. Love seemed like a distant childhood memory, something that no longer existed for me in the real world. I told myself over and over I had everything I needed, but as I stood watching myself in the mirror, I glimpsed the truth in the sorrow behind my eyes. Something stirred within me but still I resisted it.

> *no!! this is not happening*

I refused to let my need for more destroy everything I already had, but a crack formed in my beautiful life as I was given a brief impression of something else; something that promised more.

> *more real stuff, not material stuff*

My perfect life might not be as perfect as I thought and the boat began to rock. I'd been dodging feelings of discontent for years, unwilling to disrupt my life.

66

I was happy, damn it and I was staying that way.

However, this was the first time I'd fully acknowledged something might be wrong and it terrified me. I stayed in the bathroom trying to talk myself out of it. I didn't want to feel this way. I loved my husband, we had everything to be happy for and the thought of not playing the role of 'the perfect family' gave me extreme anxiety.

It's funny how in times of trauma, crazy thoughts enter your head. I began thinking about our friends. If we broke up what would happen to all of our married friends? We'd no longer be part of that set or go to couples dinners and weekends away.

> *the really important stuff that entered my head*
> *in a time of crisis.*

Feeling desperate, I pushed these thoughts to the back of my mind, took a deep breath and pulled myself together. I wasn't ready to answer these questions and I wasn't anywhere near ready to disrupt my life, so I washed my face, cleaned my teeth and went back downstairs to order my cocktail

> *Pina Colada it is then*

Jumping into the pool, I told Kevin to have a break and took over playing with the boys. Being with them made me feel better and even though my anxiety continued to rip through me, I told myself their happiness was all that mattered and mine was irrelevant. Maybe if I told myself that,

> *a few thousand times*

I'd start to believe it.

Within a couple of days and with a lot of champagne, I managed to act as if it hadn't happened and had a wonderful holiday with my family, but...something had changed. Acknowledging my unhappiness, even for a brief moment allowed years of suppressed feelings to surface and I was being bombarded. Ignoring them wasn't working anymore and distracting myself was becoming harder.

When we got home, the kids immediately went back to school and I tried to distract myself to stop thinking about the epiphany, but I had nothing to do. Maria did everything.

did I tell you she was an angel?

As well as cleaning, cooking and shopping, she was also an amazing nanny to the kids and they loved her.

we all did

Usually I'd drop the kids to school, go to the gym or come home and read, then I'd meet friends for lunch or go shopping and most days I didn't even need to pick up the kids as Maria did that if I asked her to.

sounds great doesn't it?

I was spoiled but also redundant in my own life and I despised myself for it. Everyday I awoke with nothing to do, no purpose, no interest and no job. I didn't even do charity work. At best, I got my kids up for school, but on the days when I didn't feel like it, I'd ask Maria to take them and go back to bed.

terrible mother

Then I'd lie in bed disgusted at myself for not even taking my own children to school. I had everything but I had nothing. I had an amazing lifestyle, but I didn't stop beating myself up about it. I felt guilty for the holidays we went on, guilty for the house we lived in, guilty for the cars we had and guilty for having Maria and not doing my own damn housework or taking my own kids to school.

so guilt was the overall feeling

The ultimate cliche, I was a bored housewife with a husband who worked his ass off trying to provide for his family and instead of supporting him, I was miserable and jealous of him. He was so driven, he had his career and his purpose. It was everything to him and I wanted to feel that way.

what did I have?
oh yeah an unlimited bank account,
a housekeeper, three great kids,
a fabulous lifestyle
that would make anyone unhappy!!

I thought if I got a job and had a career I loved, stupid thoughts of love being missing from my life would disappear. Why didn't I get a job and start my career again? At the time that felt impossible. I had my life with the children and financially I didn't need a job, so the motivation to get one simply wasn't there.

I'll go shopping instead and keep suppressing it!

I tried to be happy and bubbly around the children, but they were perceptive and picked up on things. They knew there was something unhappy about mummy and my relationship with my youngest son was affected the most. Unbeknown to myself,

as I was deep in the trenches of my war within

I hadn't bonded properly with him. I missed out on vital time and as a result, Sammie was a complete daddy's boy who wanted to be with his father all the time. My other sons had been mummy's boys and I found it very upsetting, adding to my feelings of guilt and failure.

As the weeks went on I thought about the epiphany I had while in Dubai: I wasn't happy. I was sad and terrified to admit love was actually missing from my life.

oh god!

Did this mean my life had to change? Did it mean my marriage was over? Kevin and I didn't really talk anymore and it was so hard pretending everything was ok. Being affectionate with him, lying next to him or making love to him felt impossible and at times I'd think, 'how can I be sleeping next to someone and feel so completely alone?'

Each morning I woke with such crippling anxiety, that I could barely breathe. Then I'd spend my day trying to push uncomfortable thoughts, feelings and emotions away. I couldn't deal with anything that pointed to the end of my marriage. A battle between my head and my heart was raging and it was tearing me apart.

I was afraid of everything, my feelings, changing my life, the effect it would have on the kids, the unknown. I wanted to stay in my perfect illusion, with my perfect life and my perfect family. I didn't want to deal with change. I hated change and would rather stick with what I had, even if it made me unhappy.

better to be unhappy than uncertain

Soon however, whether I liked it or not, change would happen. The emotions I'd pushed away for years were about to smash through to the surface of my life and I'd be forced to confront everything in the worst possible way.

8: The Book That Changed Everything

I do believe something very magical can happen when you read a good book.

- ***J K Rowling***

It was a phone call from Australia that led to the decimation of the illusion. My little sister Louise had been living there for a year and rang to tell me about a book she read, also to rub my nose in the fact that she was on a beach in Sydney while I was in cold, wet England.

bitch

On this particular morning she was very excited, "Suzanne, you need to buy this book, oh my god, it's unbelievable, get it and read it as soon as you can." As a family of readers this wasn't out of the norm for us. We're all bookworms and would regularly recommend books to each other or pass them around when we'd finished reading them. I once watched my mother hand the pages of a book she was reading to my father so he could read it as well. A good book was always up for discussion in our house and I grew up with bookstores and libraries being my favourite places. I'd spend hours walking around them looking at the books, my favourite being the library at Trinity College Dublin, one of the oldest libraries in the world.

But this book? I already knew about this book, because at the time who didn't? Everyone was going crazy for it but I had no intention of reading it and I told her so. "Read it," she urged, 'and the rest, there are four of them, you will absolutely love them." When she hung up, I didn't think about it again until she rang a couple of weeks later asking again if I'd bought them. I

72

said "no," still completely uninterested, but was out shopping the next day and happened to go into a bookstore.

no surprise as that's where I usually went

I was looking for something new to read and as I looked around the shop everything, and I mean absolutely everything, was dedicated to this book.

what the fuck?

There were posters, banners and life-size cardboard cutouts and I also noticed that every single person in the line was buying them. So with a sigh of defeat, I gave in and bought the damn books. All four of them because that's what everyone else was doing. I went home and started to read.

The book was called......

drum roll

...*Twilight* and the only words to describe what happened next were 'oh fuck.' I was a 36 year old woman, exhaustedly suppressing the feeling that love might be missing from my life and as I read these books, I knew with absolute certainty that it was. Like a tidal wave, the realisation pushed its way through and I couldn't deny it for another second.

I'd completely forgotten about love.

It hit with full force. The ground beneath me slipped away and I felt like I was falling off a cliff. By page 50 of *Twilight*, I was gone, spinning in an abyss of anguish, unable to do anything but read these books for three whole weeks. Consumed by them, I was catatonic as anxiety ripped through me. Desperate to get to the end, I couldn't think straight, I couldn't sleep, I couldn't eat and I didn't talk to anyone, because that would take me away from my reading.

Feelings I'd suppressed for years came flooding to the forefront of my mind and I was suffocating. I read as if my life depended on it, every second the kids were at school and the minute they went to bed. At last I could enjoy having my housekeeper Maria, because now I had something to do during the day.

fall apart while reading about 17 year old vampires

I thought I was in control,

I so wasn't

I thought I was hiding my feelings from everyone, my husband, Maria, my family and friends, but they all knew something was very wrong and they were very nervous. Normally I'd put on a show and convince everyone that life was great, but I couldn't do that while reading these books. When I read the last page of the last book, I was so overcome with grief that I howled for hours. I got the happy ending I desperately needed, but still I sobbed. My emotions indescribable as the illusion of my life fell away and I was walloped by the truth.

You might wonder how a book about teenage vampires can cause this to happen to a grown woman, but of course it was nothing to do with them. It was the love story that finally broke me. I realised that apart from loving my children, I hadn't ever allowed myself to experience the true emotion of love. I didn't know how to be best friends with my husband or to just love him for who he was. I'd found a way to drive my life forward by not looking too closely at it, cleaning it up and making it look perfect, while convincing myself I had everything I needed.

how the fuck did I forget about love?

I'd become emotionally suppressed and void of feelings, except superficial ones. The realisation that my whole life was based on material perfection was excruciating. I cared only about what other people thought of my life, as long as it looked perfect to everyone else, I could then convince myself that it was.

while completely ignoring the fact that I was dying inside

The true version of me, the essence of who I was, wanted me to know myself on a soul level, to live an authentic life, speak my truth, follow my dreams and fall in love with no agenda or conditions, I just didn't know how to do that.

yet

The book was my catalyst and I gained instant clarity: By trying to be the perfect wife, mother and daughter, I'd completely lost myself along the way. My dreams of love and romance had been replaced by my need for a better social standing and I felt like I'd sold my soul to the devil. For some, a traumatic event, the death of a loved one or indeed a self-help book can change their lives, but for me it was a vampire romance novel.

vampires rule!

Of course I still tried to rationalise it in my head. I loved my husband, but I now knew it wasn't a deep meaningful love, one that allowed me to feel safe and cherished, one that commanded respect, friendship and intimacy on both sides. The biggest blow was realising I couldn't love him like this, because I didn't know how to and that came from my inability to love myself.

I loathed myself. I felt unworthy of everything and had spent years trying to control my feelings and deny my emotions. I was afraid that if I actually 'let go' and people saw the real me, they'd be bitterly disappointed when they saw what I saw, a weak and broken woman, full of flaws.

and slightly chubby

I needed my life to look perfect so the people in it would love me for what I had, or what I could give them.

somebody please love me

Just being me wasn't enough, why would anyone want to be with me, unless I could impress them or give them something? Always seeking approval from others, I needed validation for simply existing and had built a cast iron wall around my heart to protect myself from being hurt. I felt alone and isolated but hadn't realised it until now and it was agony.

How does someone go through their life and not notice love is missing?

it's just the whole reason we exist

Deep down I knew, because I yearned for it; I just refused to acknowledge it and kept looking forward.

Suppress and pretend, suppress and pretend

The books woke something deep within me and I could no longer keep a lid on it. I felt none of the beautiful emotions you're supposed to feel when you're married and in love. I was mechanical, going through the motions of my life, busy proving to myself and everyone else that the poor little girl from Ireland, had made something of herself. I hadn't given myself the opportunity to choose how I truly wanted to live, because I'd had an agenda my whole damn life.

Knowing what hardship and poverty felt like, I was determined I would never feel that again. I grew up believing my only way to have a successful life was to marry someone who could achieve it.

because I certainly couldn't

My role was to plan our life, my husband's role to provide financial security, then we'd be happy, happy, happy. It never occurred to me that I could do all of that for myself. As a child when I'd float around dreaming of true love, my mother would innocently say, "Suzanne don't forget, love goes out the window when you have money problems."

ha! not happening to me, no way Jose!

She never knew a passing comment could have such an impact on my life. I'd love someone who had ambition and money, then my life would be perfect, because we'd have no money problems. Easy. Then I could just love my husband and we'd live happily ever after. The problem? Life doesn't always go to plan and I got it back to front.

I tried to manipulate my life to work in my favour, tried to force feelings that weren't there. I forgot about real love and ironically that's all I ever wanted. To love someone with all my heart and have them love me the same way.

I got everything else instead

9: Breaking Apart

Let's not forget that the little emotions are the great captains of our lives and we obey them without realising it.
- ***Vincent Van Gogh***

The day after I finished reading Twilight, I woke up in a different world and I was devastated. I knew my life had to change and cried for hours as I lay in bed, contemplating my next move with a suffocating sense of dread. When my friends and family asked what was wrong, I couldn't tell them because I didn't know.

was I going crazy? was my marriage over?

I couldn't tell Kevin either because the thought of hurting him immobilised me. I wanted to stay married, our life was amazing together, our children were happy and thriving, and I didn't want to change any of that. I wanted to love him, he was a good man, but I didn't know how to do it. Telling my girlfriends about the books, I insisted they read them and when nothing happened, I was astonished.

what the actual fuck?

Why weren't their lives falling apart like mine? I was waiting for at least one phone call and was kind of disappointed when it didn't happen. One of my girlfriends didn't even finish the first book, saying she'd found it boring.

eh...what?

My marriage had to end. I knew that but felt as if I was doing something wrong for feeling it and became paranoid someone would find out. Find out what? I didn't know. I just felt like I had to hide my feelings from everyone. My world was slipping through my fingers and I couldn't stop it. I felt ashamed of myself for feeling these things, ashamed of myself for falling apart and ashamed of myself for not being happy. I thought I should be stronger, get my shit together and stop with the drama.

just grow the fuck up Suzanne!

In the depths of my despair, I berated myself for my weakness while trying to hide my meltdown from everyone, including my husband. Crippled by negative thoughts and emotions, it felt impossible to see beyond the turmoil and then I began to wonder if I'd ever been truly happy in my life and was so horrified by that possibility that I immediately pushed it away.

nope. not going there!! no way

Retreating deep into my own world, I didn't want to see anybody. I was terrible company and part of me wanted to go back to before the books,

please take me back to pretending everything is ok

but I couldn't do it. Now that I knew, I couldn't un-know and I had to deal with that. Thankfully Kevin was working a lot; he was gone before I woke up and home after I was asleep so I was able to hide from him.

temporarily

In the mornings I'd take the kids to school and if I needed to go anywhere, I managed to become a functioning version of myself. I was the master of disguise after all and had been doing it for years, but when I was alone I fell apart. The thought of my

80

marriage ending made me feel sick. I needed the security of it to breathe. The security of having a husband, a nice home and a good lifestyle. I didn't want to be a part of the 'one in three marriages that fail' statistics. I didn't want my kids to grow up in a broken family.

what if I completely ruined their lives?

Then there were fears about my own life. What would I do? How would I manage? How would I cope alone with the kids? What if I never met anyone else and spent the rest of my life alone? What if I became poor again?

Suzanne Selvester, homeless spinster, pleased to meet you

I constantly tried to talk myself out of my problems by telling myself everything was ok, my life was amazing and I was happy.

over and over again

What if it was just me? What if my marriage was actually ok and I was just an unhappy and ungrateful bitch? Maybe if I got some help and changed who I was, my marriage would be fine and everything would be back on track. I could forget all these silly feelings and continue with my life.

yes that's it, it was all my fault

Deciding the doctor was a good place to get some sense knocked into me, I made an appointment and felt good about finally taking action. It didn't help that, my emotions were extremely unpredictable; on the morning of my appointment, I was literally falling apart. My anxiety had reached a new level and I almost crawled into the doctor's office on my knees. I begged him to help me. I couldn't keep going like this, the pain was too intense, I couldn't see straight and I felt utterly lost.

When he asked me to explain what was wrong, I just burst into tears, completely unable to describe what I felt.

> *confused, terrified, lonely, broken, paranoid, -*
> *you know just regular, upbeat kinda stuff*

Something was hurting, but I didn't know what it was. I just knew I needed help. Shocked by my emotional state, he absolutely agreed. Prescribing antidepressants and anti-anxiety tablets, he then made an appointment for me to see a psychiatrist at a London clinic two days later. He urged me to start the medication straight away, but I immediately thought about people I'd met over the years, addicted to antidepressants

> *a blue one in the morning, a green one in the afternoon*

and was afraid that would happen to me so I collected the prescription, but didn't take the tablets.

The next day my friend Bev called to see how I was. She knew to some extent what was going on and had some information she thought I might find interesting. "I saw my hairdresser today for the first time in ages," she said, "and I couldn't believe the change in her." She went on to tell me how following the sudden death of her husband, this woman had attended a clinic, similar to the one I was booked into for the past two years and hadn't seen any real progress. The change she now experienced was due to a hypnotherapist she'd been seeing for the past six weeks, something she said had completely changed her life. "Why don't you give that a go babe, before you take this medication or go to this clinic?'

a hypnotherapist?
don't they make you do stupid stuff on stage?

After some thought, I decided I hadn't taken the pills for a reason and maybe this was divine intervention, so I called and made an appointment with the hypnotherapist. If he helped this woman so much, maybe he could help me and a week later when I walked into his office, I was almost incoherent with pain. He took one look at me and his face dropped.

he was definitely going to earn his hourly rate with me

My mind was a pit of despair and I felt as if I was being sucked into a black hole, but within a few minutes of talking to him, I began to feel a little bit better. He was calm as he listened intently to what I tried to describe. He asked questions and I answered as honestly as I could, but still avoided talking about my marriage problems.

admitting it to someone else made it very real.

He finished by asking me to close my eyes for ten minutes and repeat the positive affirmation he suggested in my head. When I left him, I felt hope and what followed was nine months of excruciating therapy that tore me apart. It was like peeling an onion. Each time I had a session with him, we took off another layer until I was stripped bare and for the first time since I was a child, I opened up to someone and told them my deepest, darkest fears. It took a bit of time but some of the resentment, guilt, hurt, disappointment, fear, anxiety and worthlessness I carried on a daily basis began to ease and I felt lighter.

Together we discovered that although I came across as confident, my self-esteem was low, I didn't believe in myself and felt unworthy of everything I had. As far as I was concerned I deserved nothing and what I did have was through default. Saying it out loud helped and eventually I was forced to admit that my life with my husband was dishonest. Our life together was based on material things and my soul knew this didn't make me happy.

finally!

Although acknowledging it made me feel better, I still resisted what scared me the most and that was change itself. The unknown was my biggest enemy and it held me prisoner, but even though I was going through the biggest change of my life and my fear was destroying me. I told everyone I was fine.

I'm fine, we're fine, everything is great

Of course they didn't believe me. My friends wanted to help me, to offer compassion and understanding, but I couldn't take it. I confused compassion with pity and anyway I was a matter of fact person.

fall down, get up, brush yourself off, get over it, easy!

If someone was suffering, I could dismiss their pain as easily as I had my own for so long, or if I heard bad news I'd usually think something like, 'awe that's sad, but I'm sure they'll be fine.' I couldn't connect to anything on a deep emotional level; that was simply impossible for me. I didn't want the help and advice of my family, because I honestly thought I could shake myself out of it and stop being ridiculous.

84

stop being such a baby and get over it

Even though living with Kevin had become excruciating and everyday felt like a battlefield of constant fighting and bickering, I just got on with it. I normalised our dysfunction for so long that I didn't notice how badly we treated each other or how much disrespect we had for each other...until now. On top of that my paranoia was in full swing. I thought if Kevin found out the true extent of my feelings, he'd be gone in a puff of smoke and I couldn't let that happen. I couldn't turn to him and tell him what I was going through, I couldn't confide in him and it was killing me.

On nights when I went out with the girls, if I drank too much wine,

which was a lot of the time

I'd wake up the next day hyperventilating and terrified I'd told him the truth. I wanted to speak to him, I wanted to understand what had gone wrong between us, how we had drifted so far apart...but I just couldn't do it. Creating a story in my head, I told myself if he discovered my secret, he'd throw me out, I'd be living on the streets, he'd keep the boys from me and they'd forget who I was.

a slightly exaggerated view on the whole thing

Even though I knew it was completely irrational and wouldn't happen in a million years, I was frozen in fear. The voice in my head played the worst case scenario over and over and I couldn't see a way out. However, the change I feared so much was happening. The truth was harder to avoid and I was unable to stop it. Like water running through my fingers, soon I'd only be able to watch as the dam burst and my life changed irrevocably.

10: Big Realisations

With the new day comes new strengths and new thoughts.
- *Eleanor Roosevelt*

My lack of purpose was one of my biggest issues. For years I'd tried to convince myself I was happy just being a wife on shopping sprees and while that was very nice, it didn't fulfil me. It took me a long time to realise it was ok to want more than just being a mother. I loved my boys, they meant everything to me, but I wanted to achieve something for myself. When I had worked in the past I'd gone from job to job, convincing myself that each one was it, only to get bored after three months and leave, never knowing what I wanted to do and exhausted trying to figure it out.

My marriage problems however were my priority and something I could no longer avoid. The disrespect Kevin and I had for each other had to stop. If he was disrespectful to me, instead of discussing it with him, I was equally as disrespectful to him.

challenge accepted!

Certain aspects of his personality would never change, but I just couldn't accept that about him and used it against him. He mainly saw the negative in a situation and he was very controlled. He got upset about situations that to me were completely irrelevant, like running out of milk or not putting something back in its correct place.

jeez, get over it

I was the opposite and our relationship was a constant battle. If there was something in particular I wanted, his immediate response was no and he'd lecture me on why that wasn't a good idea. A holiday destination could be discussed for hours. If I wanted to go somewhere in particular, it was a bad idea. He'd book something else and because it was always something fabulous, I told myself I should be grateful.

I wasn't being heard

If I wanted some work done in the house, I was being ridiculous and it was impossible. It would get done eventually, but on his terms and slightly different to what I wanted. Again, I'd tell myself he was an engineer and knew better.

I still wasn't being heard

If I said black, he said white and over the years he wore me down. Living with him was exhausting and I was tired of fighting. Before my therapy I was happy for him to have control, but now I wanted some of it back. I wanted to make some decisions about the things we did as a family.

I envied my girlfriends who were responsible for their family finances. I didn't even pay a bill and although it was done with good intentions, I felt smothered and useless. The less I did, the more useless I felt and Kevin often made fun of me by calling me useless and lazy. He said he meant it in a lighthearted way, but each time it destroyed another little piece of me, because that's exactly how I felt and hearing it out loud only made it worse.

Of course, I didn't tell him any of this.

don't be stupid, that would be far too sensible

I just banked it in my huge bank of resentment to use against him as future ammunition. I didn't tell him his comments were hurtful or that every time he called me useless, it cut me to the bone. I just slung insults back at him, terrified to show my vulnerability and thus allowing my resentment and blame to build. He was my husband, but we were a million miles apart. I didn't know how to be honest and connect with him and the longer it went on, the more impossible it seemed.

Maybe if I'd talked to him, we could have worked on it, but I was so full of self-loathing and self-sabotage that when he pushed, I just pushed back.

take that asshole

Talking to him about my feelings or asking for help, didn't even cross my mind. At times I felt like he despised me, because ultimately, I despised myself. He only saw the negative in me, but equally as guilty, I only saw the negative in him.

A clean house was his obsession. Now throw in three small boys and a naturally untidy wife and you can imagine how that went. One particular Friday when the children were younger and before we had Maria. I had cleaned the house from top to bottom and it was immaculate. I sat the kids in front of the TV all afternoon, telling them I wanted the house to look nice for Daddy and even towel dried the floor on my hands and knees to make it shine, because he liked it that way. Just before he came home, I rushed around throwing all the washing and cleaning products into the utility room and closed the door, to sort later. He was home five minutes, got changed upstairs and brought his washing down.

Walking into the utility room, he immediately began shouting about the state of it, "Jesus Suzanne, this house is a shit hole, what the hell do you do all day?" I just stood gaping at him.

as in mouth open in a fish like manner

Was he serious? He was and I was devastated. Of course a massive argument followed and the surprise was ruined. It seemed no matter what I did, I could never please him and earn his praise. I was twelve years old again, looking for the same love and approval from my father and I still wasn't getting it from my husband. He couldn't see what I did for him, only what I didn't do and living with that every day was killing me.

My easygoing, relaxed and untidy nature grated on him. I often stepped out of my clothes and left them on the floor. They got picked up eventually, but I lacked his urgency for neatness. I was disorganized. I never knew where anything was and could spend half an hour looking for a pair of scissors which drove him insane.

I ran a very tight shipwreck

A fly by the seat of my pants, it always worked out in the end, kind of girl, there was a big clash of personalities. If we disagreed on something, he felt the need to discuss every single detail, asking question after question, while I was dying of boredom and almost asleep. Somewhere along the line, I gave up fighting him, it was too hard, so I just went along with whatever he wanted for a peaceful life.

I knew if there was something I really wanted I could get him to think it was his idea but that in itself was completely dysfunctional. It wasn't a partnership, an honest, loving relationship, it was a stupid game of trying to get one over on each other. "I'm trying to make your life easier," he'd say when I'd tell him to stop nagging at me.

oh just fuck off

He thought I should be more organised and more efficient and would tell me ways to do that, but I didn't want to hear it. I already knew I was disorganised, lazy and inefficient and having it thrown in my face day after day did nothing to change that. I already felt like I was doing a bad job of everything, adding to my already huge sense of failure. I didn't need any more.

If we were out with friends, the disrespect got worse. For some reason, we had to tear each other apart in front of everyone. If I was talking about something or telling a story, he'd interrupt me constantly. 'Don't be so stupid, it wasn't like that,' or 'you're completely exaggerating Suzanne, that didn't happen.'

I speak in hyperbole, what can I say!

It was excruciating, making everyone feel uncomfortable, and I'd usually respond by slagging him off or getting drunk and flirting with other guys in front of him. I was desperate, attention seeking and in excruciating pain. Mix it together with white wine and I hardly recognise the girl I was, a girl so desperate for love and so completely lost.

somebody help me please!

As my therapy progressed, my marriage continued to limp along but I was completely unravelling and I could no longer pretend I was ok. Even though I tried to be happy around them, my children knew something was wrong. As soon as they went to bed, I'd open one,

sometimes two

bottles of wine, because getting smashed off my face helped me avoid the reality of my life. If Kevin was home, I'd go out with my friends and leave him to babysit.

One day my therapist asked me to write a list of good things about me and I laughed.

good things? ha!! don't be ridiculous man

The idea seemed so alien to me, I only saw what I lacked in my life, in my personality, in my body shape, in the bedroom, in the kitchen, as a mother, as a wife, as a woman. It felt strange to consider the possibility of anything good but I decided to have a go and thought about it for a while.

Eventually I came up with a couple of things; I knew I had a nice face and could pull off pretty, I could be the life and soul of a party and I was a good mother to my sons.

there, that wasn't too hard, was it?

Thinking about it more, other good things began to spring to mind and then something strange happened. The more I focused on the positive things about me, the more positive I began to feel.

I'm a fairly kind person, I often consider the needs of others.

ok, that was another one, I could do this

I read people well and picked up on the emotions of a situation or a person very quickly. I'm generous.

it was getting harder but I kept going

Soon my list began to grow; I'm smart, I can be funny, I'm interesting, sometimes. I'm determined, when I put my mind to something, I usually do it. The floodgates opened and I began to see myself in a different light.

maybe I wasn't that bad after all

In the following months, my perspective began to shift. I asked myself why I felt so ashamed of my marriage problems? Why did I need to hide my feelings from Kevin and everyone else? People have marriage problems every day. Things go wrong and that's ok. Couples talk about their problems and either overcome them or split up and that was ok too. Had I created a monster in my head?

a very big, angry monster

Very slowly I was overcoming my irrational fear of exposure and accepting that my life might be about to change. I felt ready to reach out to the people in my life and ask for help, something that seemed impossible only a few months before. The secrecy and isolation I imposed on myself

because of my shame, the more shame I felt,
the more I needed to hide

began to fade and with the help of my therapist, I finally wanted to open up about my marriage problems. However, by now there

93

was another secret in my life that I absolutely could not share with anyone and it was eating me alive.

11: Shame & Humiliation

Shame is a soul eating emotion.
-    *C G Jung*

Finally telling my friends and family about my marriage problems was no surprise to anyone. They already knew! Following months of overthinking, I came clean and guess what? No one cared. I hadn't done anything bad after all. They just wanted to help and support me and it felt so good to finally talk about it. Having their opinion and support was brilliant and I couldn't believe I'd gone through so much alone.

why was I hiding it again?

What they didn't know, what no one could ever know was that we were also having serious financial difficulties. It was 2008, the recession had hit hard and my husband's business was in construction. Everything was going wrong.

Now, here's the thing....when you already have marriage problems and you add money problems to the mix, the shit really hits the fan. Kevin was under ridiculous pressure every single day and totally consumed in trying to save his business. He worked constantly and we saw less and less of each other. My girlfriends became my lifeline and I clung to them desperately. Although my family in Dublin knew about my marriage problems, they didn't know the extent of them, and I was okay with that.

my Catholic shame threatened to rise up
and swallow me whole

95

Our money worries took my shame to the next level and I was horrified at the idea of being poor again and losing everything, as we'd done when Sean was born. What if I had another asthma attack, what if this one killed me? The washing machine in my stomach churned every minute of every day. Kevin had a make or break investor lined up, someone who could fix everything, but the whole process took so long and while we waited for news, we lived on a knife edge.

Being able to talk about my marriage problems however, distracted me from the financial ones.

so I started talking and I didn't stop

If anyone asked how I was, instead of saying I was ok as I'd done in the past, I'd tell the truth and soon everyone knew. The girls at the gym knew, the people in the queue at Sainsbury's knew, the doctor's receptionist knew, the milkman, the postman and anyone else I talked to in my day. If you brought it up, I talked about it. If you didn't bring it up, I still talked about it, desperate for someone to tell me it was going to be okay.

Sharing it was me accepting the fact that my marriage might be over. Very slowly

and I mean super slowly

I was taking responsibility for my feelings and finally admitting how I truly felt. All I needed to do now was tell Kevin, something that terrified me. The atmosphere between us was abominable and it was affecting the kids badly. When Kevin was home, we were fighting, when he was at work, we were fighting by text. He was out of his mind with money worries, I was out of my mind with money worries. He was sleeping in the spare room so we had no physical contact, no support for each other, no intimacy, no affection, no nothing. The only thing we had in our life was stress, fear, worry and loneliness.

I had the loneliness, I don't think he had time for that

With all this going on, I couldn't tell him we needed to talk about our marriage problems as well. Talk about kicking him when he was down.

lovely! another excuse not to talk

Things came to a head on the night of his 40th birthday. We had a fancy dress party at home and I was determined it would be great. Even though money was tight, we hired caterers, booked a DJ, and welcomed our guests together. One hundred and fifty people in our house, all having a great time. Kevin was happy and relaxed for the first time in months, but what happened that night was so destructive to our marriage that even writing about it gives me anxiety.

Before I continue, please remember that when love and affection are missing from your life, you look for it everywhere.

and I looked for it everywhere

I'd watch other couples interacting and wish I had some of that. I'd dream of being in love, I wanted to feel that so badly. Desperately unhappy, alone and scared, I was tired of fighting with Kevin and tired of being miserable all the time, so when a single friend of Kevin's arrived at the party, I was happy to see him.

very happy to see him

We'd always had a flirty relationship which Kevin encouraged, all harmless fun under normal circumstances, but our circumstance was far from normal. I can only surmise that I temporarily lost my mind that night because the minute he arrived, I made a beeline for him and came on strong.

all over him

He looked worried, but I didn't care. I was already tipsy and in complete self-destruct mode as my need for attention overrode my sanity and I hung onto his every word. My friends of course noticed and tried to pull me away, but the alcohol was running through my veins and I paid no attention to any of them. When it got very late and most people left, I stripped off into my bra and knickers and jumped into the hot-tub in our garden.

as if that was a perfectly normal thing to do at 5am

The few hardcore friends still partying followed me, my husband and his friend included, and it took me five-seconds to pounce on him. I was all over him, hugging and kissing him, completely oblivious to my husband and his other friends talking and drinking in the tub behind me. A combination of emotional chaos, ten hours of drinking cocktails and champagne and I resembled something close to a car crash. The true feelings I'd been hiding from everyone, particularly my husband came flooding out of my mouth.

like the verbal vomit express for everyone to hear

In between kissing and hugging him, I told him how bored I was in my marriage, how I craved something more from a man and how much I fancied him. I told him he stimulated my mind and

98

that I thought about him all the time. I kept going on and on and the whole time Kevin

and everyone else in the hot-tub

listened to every word I said. Revealing my true feelings, I was exposed and in the worst possible way. He'd known it was bad, but to hear it like that, on his birthday, in front of his friends, from his wife who forgot he was even there was utterly humiliating. As far as I was concerned it was just me and his friend in the hot-tub as I bared my soul to him.

When I opened my eyes the next morning, as well as a humdinger of a hangover, I was in complete shock. The memories came flooding back, my worst fear was realised and I wanted to die. Frozen to my pillow, I knew I'd crossed a line and when I looked across the room and saw Kevin standing at the door with a look of complete disgust on his face, I was deeply ashamed of myself.

Leaving the room without a word, he went downstairs to entertain our friends who had come back for brunch. I pulled myself together and finally went down, but he was busy cooking BBQ and drinking beer again. People came and went throughout the day and they couldn't help but notice the tension between us. With each beer Kevin drank, his aggression towards me increased and our biggest argument ever followed that night and even though I knew it was coming, I was unprepared for the force of it.

He was devastated and hated me for what I'd done. I'd publicly humiliated him and I couldn't take it back. He screamed his disgust at me, I screamed back at him, the children were crying, my mother was crying, it was awful and probably the darkest moment in our whole marriage.

I wanted to curl up and die. I hated myself. What the fuck was wrong with me?

you were in a lot of pain

Where was my self respect,

you had none

my dignity?

nope, none of that either

Why couldn't I just tell him how I felt instead of getting drunk, revealing the truth and making myself look like a complete fucking bitch. The pain and guilt I lived with for months, the worry I had about hurting him became irrelevant, because I drank too much and hurt him in the worst possible way.

As I predicted many months before, the minute he found out, he was off. The next morning he said he was leaving, he was going to pack a bag and move out. If that's how I felt, he didn't see any point in sticking around and I had to beg him to talk about it. Hyperventilating and crying, I didn't want to let him go, but I knew I wasn't in love with him. I wanted my marriage to end, but I also didn't want it to end. Now that he knew about my feelings, surely we had to discuss our next move, even for the sake of the kids.

100

He agreed to go for lunch while my mother took care of the kids and we put all our cards on that table. I apologised from the bottom of my heart for my behaviour because no matter how bad our relationship was, he didn't deserve that. He accepted my apology and we finally started talking to each other. I told him about reading Twilight and the effect it had on me. I told him about my fear and some of my feelings. I wasn't completely honest, I didn't tell him I wasn't in love with him anymore, I told him I was trying to work it all out in my head which was partly true, but at least we were talking and that was progress.

Acknowledging our marriage problems seemed to help. I was no longer alone in my turmoil and by the end of lunch, we'd talked to each other more than we had in years. I started remembering the old version of us and after a few hours of talking, we both decided to give it one more try. I ignored the voice in my head screaming at me to stop wasting my time.

oh for fuck sake, this is your way out

It was telling me I was trying to force feelings that just weren't there, but my life would be easier if I stayed married so I needed to do that. Maybe it would change, maybe I could fall in love with him again, maybe we could be happy and make it work.

maybe pigs will fly

I opened up about my feelings of uselessness, my need for achievement and fulfilment. He immediately organised for me to meet and work with one of his colleagues on a particular project. He encouraged me to get involved and even gave me a desk at his London office. I felt like I had something else to do and working again felt great. I'd go to the office a couple of times a week, working and interacting with other people. Suddenly my marriage problems didn't seem so big anymore. I had other things to focus on and realised how much I'd missed it.

Maria was taking care of the kids and I was busy with a number of projects for people in Kevin's office and I loved it. I'd go to the deli on the corner for my sandwich at lunchtime and if Kevin was around, he'd take me for a nice lunch. We had a common interest, we could discuss work and I felt happier. I'd succeeded in convincing myself that we might actually make it.

again

However, being at the office and interacting with people, allowed something else to become very apparent. I noticed that when people spoke to me, I couldn't hear them. I ignored it at first because I knew exactly what was happening and was doing the usual... denying it. My family had a medical condition of premature hearing loss and all the signs were pointing to me going deaf. I kinda knew my hearing was on the decline for sometime, but hoped I was wrong.

When I was younger, the idea of losing my hearing was brilliant, something else to make me stand out, but now that it might be happening, I was shit scared and absolutely did not want it. Deciding to face it head on, I booked an appointment to see an audiologist and when he confirmed that my hearing was indeed in decline, I was devastated. You have got to be kidding me, I was in my mid-thirties, struggling to save my marriage and raise my kids, going through deep financial crisis, trying to figure out who I was and what I wanted to do with my life. Now I was going deaf?

anything else?

I told Kevin my results and he wasn't surprised. He'd already suspected as he had to say everything at least twice for me to hear him. His support meant a lot to me and convinced me more than ever that we might be back on track. I was now working, I was confiding in my husband and he was listening. I thought, maybe, just maybe it might all work out in the end.

always the optimist

12: A New York State of Mind

New York, New York. So good they named it twice.
- ***Frank Sinatra***

A couple of weeks before Christmas I flew to New York with my girlfriends for a well needed break and some Christmas shopping. The trip had been booked long before our financial situation deteriorated so we decided I should still go. My marriage had been back on track for six weeks and I was trying,

really trying

but the feeling of inevitability had returned with full force. Deep down I knew I was flogging a dead horse, but I just couldn't face the pain of going through a marriage breakdown. The thought of it sent me into a frenzy of panic and I wanted it all to go away.

When we arrived at Heathrow, a surprise upgrade to business class gave us a great start to the weekend. As we sat in our business class seats, sipping champagne and chatting about life,

mostly mine

love and everything we wanted to buy that weekend. My closest girlfriends knew about my situation and their support was my lifeline. Long dog walks had seen us hash it all out, go through several options and discuss worst case scenarios. They helped me more than any therapy I'd had over the years and each had a very different opinion on my predicament. Catherine,

who I moved to London to live with all those years before

was easygoing, great fun and happily married. She listened without saying too much, usually letting me work it out on my own and when I finally shut up, she'd offer some great insight. She liked Kevin very much and would have liked us to stay together, but she also thought if I wasn't happy, I should leave.

Sensible advice

Kate who at the time was unsure about her own marriage and didn't need anything highlighting the fact that she had potential problems.

something she told me some years later

She had a reserved point of view and thought I should do everything I could to make it work. "A marriage needs to be worked on," she'd say and she was right, it did but I couldn't help wonder if mine was beyond that. I quickly realised people can only give advice based on their own experience. These girls were the best therapy. I loved them and wouldn't have survived without their help.

Girl Power

New York was five days of complete madness. My cousins from Ireland were barmen in Manhattan and more cousins from Ireland were visiting the same weekend.

carnage

We partied hard and did absolutely no Christmas shopping. Hitting every bar and club we could find, none of us got to bed before 6am each morning. On the last day, we all decided to stay in the hotel room for some much needed sleep, but I wasn't quite ready to quit just yet. When I drank, I really drank, so pointing to a pub on the corner from our hotel window, I said to the girls, "I'll be in there," and five minutes later, I walked into The Nancy Whiskey on Canal Street in Tribeca and smiled.

It was packed with Christmas parties and because I'd been drinking all weekend, the party girl version of Suzanne immediately clicked into place as I ordered a bottle of Budweiser.

line 'em up bartender!

A couple of hours later, my hangover was gone and everyone in the bar was my new best friend. I was deep in conversation with a man I'd just met. He was very tall, Greek/American, full of interesting chat and I'd never talked to anyone quite like him before. We sat in the pub for hours and I poured my heart out to him. I told him what I hadn't told anyone else, my deepest secrets, my deepest fears and how I really felt about my marriage.

just the usual lighthearted Christmas cheer!

This poor guy had come for a pint and was now getting the complete lowdown on my marriage problems. I don't know why I was so open with him, maybe it was because he was a stranger and I was drinking, or maybe it was because I was feeling emotionally vulnerable and needed to vent. Whatever the case, I just kept talking and he just kept listening, offering his opinion here and there.

When I finally shut up, he didn't say much for a few minutes and then offered me a completely different perspective which was this: What about me?

106

eh, what?

What about my happiness in all of this?

what's that got to do with anything?

Wasn't there the possibility of a bright side?

a bright side? what's that?

It seemed to him that I was trying very hard to make everything ok based on my fear. My fear of hurting my husband, my fear of ruining my children's lives, my fear of what my friends and family would think, my fear of being alone. As far as he could see, I was overlooking the most important question which was, what about me? What about my happiness in all of this?

well knock me on my ass with a feather!

Was I happy right now, would I be happy if I stayed in this marriage? Would my husband be happy if he stayed married to a woman who didn't love him? Would my kids be happy with a mother who was spiraling into depression? Would they be happy with parents who fought all the time?

no to all of the above

I just stared at him as he asked these questions, completely blown away. He'd put a different spin on it and as I sat with my mouth open, my life flashed before my eyes. If I wasn't happy now, how could I be happy if things didn't change? How could I raise my kids to be happy if their mother was sad? If they grew up thinking the relationship I had with their father was love, they'd have a distorted version of love and I'd be responsible for that.

Floored by this conversation, I was still trying to process it when the girls showed up. They had a taxi outside and it was time to go to the airport. For a split second, I was tempted to stay. I wanted to talk more, but of course that wasn't possible, so I gave him my email address, said goodbye and really hoped I'd hear from him again.

Halfway across the Atlantic, I woke from a restless sleep and found myself thinking about the anxiety and fear I lived with for so long. Could I honestly go from being so desperately unhappy, so certain my marriage was over, to everything being fine again? I knew I was in deep denial, but that seemed easier than ending my marriage.

When I arrived back in the UK, it took a week for my body to recover. I was exhausted from lack of sleep, toxic with alcohol poisoning and when the effects wore off? I nose dived into a cavern of emotional chaos as anxiety ripped through me. However, I was also thinking about the conversation I had with the American in the bar. A simple shift in perspective had changed my mindset and I absolutely knew my marriage had to end.

I just had to break the news to Kevin

I kept in touch with my American friend through email and a few weeks later we began talking on Skype. Suddenly there was someone in my life offering an objective point of view. He thought I was one of the most interesting women he'd ever met. He said I was beautiful, with amazing energy and a dynamic personality.

wow, me? you're talking about me?

I didn't know what to do with that, I'd never been told it in such an elegant way before.

The answer to his question from the bar was no I wouldn't be happy if I stayed in my marriage and neither would Kevin. Before we knew it, another couple of months had passed and things were slipping again. I was tired of pretending everything was ok. I was tired of not feeling good enough, I was tired of being scared, I'd say the wrong thing and give myself away and I'd long forgotten that loving somebody was supposed to feel good.

The feelings I had when I'd read Twilight two years earlier slammed into me with full force. Love was still missing from my life. I was another year older and I still hadn't done anything about it. I wanted love, I missed it. Was I to go another ten years before I did anything? Was I to continue in a semi state of happiness, pretending that everything was ok while missing out on the beautiful gift of love? My time with my husband was strained and awkward and if we did have sex which wasn't often, I felt nothing.

Kevin was gorgeous, but I had no desire for him, I didn't fancy him anymore. He was a great guy, an amazing father, but any attraction I had to him was gone and I loathed myself for not walking away. The time had come. I was ready to come clean, I had to end the marriage but as fate would have it, I didn't get the chance. The day after I made this decision, he took matters into his own hands.

13: The Inevitable End

The end is just a new beginning.
- *J Stanford*

As I sat frozen in panic, looking at the two pieces of paper in my husband's hand, I felt like I was going to throw up. Two white A4 sheets, one listing 'everything I was doing wrong' in our marriage and the other completely blank. This was it, his ultimatum and his breaking point. As if in slow motion, he lifted one hand and waved the first sheet, "We can do this the hard way Suzanne and discuss everything on this list or," waving the other one said "we can do it the easy way and end this marriage right now." My first thought apart from being sick was, 'oh fuck, here it is.' I'd known this was coming for quite some time and was hoping our problems would just go away and disappear, but here it was staring me in the face and all I could do was stare back at it, incapable of responding.

He'd beaten me to it, I'd finally found the courage to end the marriage and my grand plan was foiled by Kevin coming home from work to do it himself. There was no going back and throughout the whole conversation, my emotions were all over the place as the tears rolled down my face. I felt panic, fear and relief all at the same time, but I knew it was the right thing to do.

the only thing harder than leaving was staying

It had to break and maybe one day it could be fixed, but for now,

one week before our 12th wedding anniversary

it broke and my heart broke along with it.

111

No longer being together after nearly 15 years felt so strange. The days that followed our breakup saw two strangers living in the same house. We tiptoed around each other, unsure of how to behave. One day married with the right to shout and scream at each other, the next day, not sure what to say or do. I wanted him gone so I could think clearly and he felt the same way. Together we looked for a new house for him and when the kids spent their first weekend there, I fell apart.

My kids were gone. My babies would be missing mummy and I wasn't there. I wanted to visit, to see how they were doing in their new, part time home, but I deliberately stayed away. They needed some space to figure it out and so did I. Dragging my girlfriends to the pub, in between glasses of wine, I bawled like a baby.

drinking myself into oblivion probably
wasn't the best way to figure anything out

The voice in my head tormented me. 'What have you done? How could you let a man like that go? You'll never find anyone like him again.'

When the boys came back on Sunday evening, my panic receded. They were my anchor and as we all said goodbye to daddy, I thought wow, how quickly we'd become a separated family. As the weeks went on, they didn't really notice daddy wasn't home at night. I had to let Maria go because we could no longer afford to pay her and with another broken heart, I said goodbye to my dear friend.

Being back in control of my own home was good for me, having things to do, even if it was just taking the kids to school and cleaning my own house. It gave me the sense of purpose I needed. Kevin popped in for dinner with the boys at least once a week and we were usually at the rugby club together on Sunday morning, regardless of who's weekend it was. Soon things began to flow, I felt more peaceful and noticed the sense of dread I'd become used to was easing. The weight of the world was lifting from my shoulders and it felt good.

Although I still wanted to discover my purpose,

> *I was born to do something,*
> *I just had no idea what it was*

the kids were my priority and I had to make sure they were okay. Constantly worried about how they'd cope, I tried to be more present and more engaging to make up for daddy not being there. My heart broke sometimes when Sammie would ask where his daddy was; being only five years old, he kept forgetting he was gone.

Part of me was overwhelmed by the realisation I'd faced something huge in my life and survived it. For years, I thought our breakup would kill me and here I was alive and kicking and ready to embrace this new chapter in my life. I wanted my kids to grow up knowing they were loved by a happy and fulfilled mother.

> *I just didn't know how to be her yet*

A few months passed and our financial situation got worse by the minute. I tried to ignore the sense of impending doom and prayed it would turn out okay. One weekend when Kevin had taken the boys to see his family, I used some of the thousands of air miles I'd collected over the years to go to New York for a few days. I told myself I was getting away from it all, but secretly I wanted to see my friend again as he'd been amazingly supportive throughout my breakup and I was curious. Could he be something more than a friend?

We spent time together in New York, walking around Manhattan, taking pictures, drinking coffee and hitting the Irish bars. Free of the anxiety that my marriage might be coming to an end, it was wonderful to be there and a small part of me hoped that perhaps I'd met my soulmate in this man,

> *anything to avoid being alone,*
> *scared and losing everything*

but spending time with him made me realise that wasn't the case, he was definitely just a friend.

Disappointed, I returned to London to face the reality of life alone. At this point in my life, I didn't know my happiness lived within me and that I was safe and loved. I didn't know that all love starts with self-love and so I looked everywhere for love. I wanted to fall in love.

> *to be safe and happy*

I wanted to be in a relationship.

> *to be safe and happy*

I wanted to find my purpose.

> *to be safe and happy*

I wanted more money.

to be safe and happy

I desperately pursued everything in my life, constantly seeking all of these things and unable to appreciate what I already had. As time went on, my emotional state became somewhat fragile because none of the above were coming to me. I was alone, with no clue as to what I was going to do with my life and broke. Some days I felt strong and optimistic, convinced everything I wanted was just around the corner. Other days, I was so overcome with fear and loneliness, I could barely get out of bed.

Kevin was hands-on and that meant I had lots of free time to cope with the rollercoaster of emotions without the children witnessing too much of it. I got used to handing them over every other Friday night. I knew they were safe with their father and if I really wanted to see them, I'd pop over for a cup of tea or go to dinner with them as my relationship with Kevin allowed for that.

My weekends off were usually spent falling apart and getting smashed off my face with my single girlfriends.

more wine anyone?

There was always someone to go out with and I couldn't be home alone. I had a sense of urgency and desperately wanted to meet someone before Kevin did. The idea that he would fall in love before me was too much to take and a race in my mind began.

I was unaware that I liked creating pain

115

I told myself Kevin would find happiness because he deserved it and I'd be left on the shelf forever, an old spinster, never to find love again.

On the upside, at least I could socialise without anxiety. I no longer had to worry about going home, having drank too much wine and saying something I'd regret in the morning. Dublin became my safe haven, I wanted to be close to my family, even though being in Ireland as a 'soon to be divorced woman' felt strange. My family was devastated by my marriage ending and couldn't understand why. "He's such a good man, a good father and a good provider," my mother would say, "why would you let that go?"

because I didn't love him enough

I didn't know how to answer her questions and it caused me a lot of anxiety. I felt so guilty, so confused and so uncertain about everything. It took a few years, but my mother eventually told me she understood why and thought I was very brave.

which meant a lot to me

Before we knew it, a year had passed and Kevin and I both accepted there was no going back. I still suffered with extreme anxiety on a daily basis and was constantly worried about my life, but things were about to change, I just had to dive a little further in chaos before they did.

14: Inescapable Bankruptcy

Three things can not be long hidden.
The sun, the moon and the truth.
- ***The Buddha***

Kevin was in my life and I was in his. That meant the kids had a gentle introduction to divorce. We often took them out together for dinner or trips to the cinema, but our friendship was delicate and we were both still in a lot of pain.

About a year after our breakup, I had builders in my house doing some urgent repairs. They all worked for Kevin so he was outside telling them what to do and left his laptop open on my kitchen table, something he never did.

ohhhhh!! no I can't....but

I couldn't help myself as I inched my way towards it in a stealth like manner. My old insecurity immediately kicked in and I found myself looking through his emails. I didn't know what I was looking for, but I knew I was supposed to see something.

the anxiety monster inside me
was screaming for more pain

Completely disgusted at myself,

not really

I scrolled to the bottom of his emails and when I saw a name I recognized. I felt physically sick. At the beginning of my marriage when I was really insecure, I used to look for proof of Kevin's infidelity. I unknowingly needed to confirm my sense

117

of worthlessness and top up on my self-loathing. But we weren't together anymore. This was none of my business and even though I knew that and even though I tried not to, I clicked on the email.

ahhh that's better

It dated back to the time when Kevin and I had just broken up

like two weeks after we'd broken up

and I couldn't quite believe what I was reading. It was very clear from the content of the email that he'd fallen in love and had a brief, but intense love affair and I was paralysed.

what the fuck?

Every word I read proved he'd gone straight from our marriage into a relationship with another woman while I tore myself apart with guilt.

As I scrolled through all the emails, my feeling of nausea increased by the second. How could he do this? I felt so betrayed, so hurt and even though we'd split up by then, it felt like he'd cheated on me. When he came back into the kitchen I tried to coerce the truth from him. I lied and told him I'd heard about this relationship from someone we both knew and he completely denied it. He lied back to me; he said it never happened

you sneaky little liar... like me

When I told him I'd read his email, his face dropped and he could no longer deny it. First he shouted at me, told me I had no right to invade his privacy but I didn't care, I was so pissed off and screamed at him. "Why the fuck didn't you tell me? I've been drowning in guilt since our marriage ended and you fell in love."

much to the builders amusement

He said it was none of my business and in that moment I realised something very important, but I'll get to that in a minute.

He eventually told me everything. "It only went on for a few weeks," he said and when he told me she broke his heart, I was mortified. She broke your heart?

what the fuck

Did I break your heart? Did you even give a shit that our marriage ended? Was all the pain and guilt I went through irrelevant? I felt so deceived by him. We were still on our agreed six month trial separation and he'd moved on straight away. I thought about my escape to New York into what I hoped was the arms of my soulmate, but that was different. I hadn't fallen in love.

but you really wanted to

My inner victim needed to bask in the glory of this pain and I was fucking pissed off.

We talked about it, he apologised and admitted he should have told me, I knew her and was bound to find out about it which might have been awkward. Surprisingly I found myself confessing my intentions while in New York and when he said he'd already suspected there was someone attracting me back there, the realisation I had before was confirmed and it was this:

119

when our marriage ended, it completely ended for both of us. There was no six month trial separation, we both moved on straight away, me emotionally and him physically and emotionally. I'd beaten myself up with guilt for nothing and suddenly I felt free of it.

Of course I tried to get more details about his relationship

purely for gossiping rights

but he wouldn't share. We decided if we were going to be friends, we had to accept the idea of other people being in our lives, but knowing how easily my husband had moved on hurt me. He'd been disrespectful and dishonest with me, but when I thought about it, I'd been equally as disrespectful and dishonest with him by going to New York.

When Kevin left, I felt quite excited at the prospect of dating someone, but exactly one week later, he turned up at my front door again and dropped the biggest bombshell of all, one I wasn't sure I'd survive.

I was studying at home, as part of a stress management course I was doing. Trying to find direction in my life, I thought educating myself was a good start and eventually wanted to start my own business. When Kevin turned up I instinctively knew something was wrong. A *deja vu* moment of him walking up the stairs carrying a cardboard box, ten years earlier hit me and, trying not to panic, I made some tea. He got straight to the point, "I've just been declared bankrupt," he said and although I heard the words, I was falling as the floor beneath me disappeared and once again my world came crashing down.

All the deals he'd worked on and all the stress he'd been under trying to save his business for the past eighteen months had been a waste of time and he was devastated. I'd known it was bad and had been worried, but I didn't know how bad. I thought he'd sorted it out and deliberately didn't ask because I just couldn't deal with it on top of everything else.

When he told me he'd used our life savings to pay his employee's wages for the past six months, I nearly threw up. We now had nothing and even though I tried not to be completely selfish and worry only about the impact it had on our family, that's exactly what I felt. We had three kids, mortgage, cars, school fees and so on.

He told me everything and I remained calm.

been there, done that, had the T-shirt

I reassured him that everything would be ok. I was outwardly positive but trembling on the inside. We'd recover from this, we'd done it before and we'd do it again. When he went into even more detail however, I couldn't breathe. He owed a lot of money and we were stone cold broke. Everything would have to be sold. Our cars, our jewellery, our house, everything.

"We can sell the cars straight away to keep the wolves from the door," Kevin said. He had a number of Cartier watches and I had a few bits and pieces, but my prized possession was worth the most. The ring from Dubai, the one I'd gotten for our 10th wedding anniversary and I loved it. It was worth a lot of money and Kevin gave me a choice. I could keep the ring and we'd take the children out of school and put them into a local one, or I could sell the ring and pay the school fees.

no pressure then!

How could I take them out of school when I had a way of keeping them there? They'd already been through so much, to take them out of a school they loved, away from all their friends was heartbreaking and I couldn't do it. So with tears rolling down my face, I handed over my beautiful ring to Kevin, he sold it and the kids got to stay in school.

The house was the next thing to go and having already lost my home many years before, I knew how this went. I'd move into rented accommodation with the kids, he'd pay off the debt incurred trying to save the business and we'd be home free.

with nothing to show for it.

At this stage, I didn't care. I went into survival mode and knew that whatever had to be done, had to be done. I refused to let my emotional attachment to the house or my insecurity about money take over because if I did, I'd start crying and I wouldn't stop.

It took six months for Kevin to earn enough money for us to breathe again. During that time the house was for sale and we were living on a small amount of money. Every time I went grocery shopping, I'd nervously watch the total adding up on the checkout screen, sweating and praying that my bank card would be approved.

please, please, please...phew

I tried to get a job, but I had the wrong experience and the kids had to be picked up at different times throughout the day; then there were after school sports clubs, swimming lessons and rugby training. One parent needed to be available and Kevin was working 24/7 so we both agreed it had to be me.

Mortified at the thought of being poor again, I didn't tell anyone the extent of our problems and did the only thing I could think of to keep up appearances, applied for credit cards. Like winning the lottery, every time I applied and got approved, I felt like the money had been given to me and gave no thought to paying it back. Kevin gave me whatever he had, a bit of money here and there, so I supplemented our life with the cards. Before I knew it, I'd run up over thirty thousand pounds of debt and when the bills came in, I had to use one card to pay the other which eventually spiraled out of control and ruined my credit rating for years.

This was the rock bottom point in my life; everything had come crashing down and I was drowning in fear. My marriage was over, we lost everything, I didn't know who I was, I was separated, a single mother trying to raise her boys. I had no money, a shit load of debt and no sense of purpose.

life had really come together for me!!

All my fears were realised at once and some days I was so full of terror I could barely put one foot in front of the other. Other days, I felt like this was pushing me towards something else. Forcing me to take responsibility for my own life but whatever the case, that's all I could do. It was sink or swim and I didn't have the option of sinking. I had three little boys to take care of, so I had to swim.

I had to move forward and was determined to find myself and at least try to be happy. Having spent my life searching for happiness in external things, when I got everything I wanted, I realised there was no happiness in any of it. Now I'd lost everything and still no happiness. The time had come to try something new, to find this happiness somewhere else. I just had to figure out how to do that.

Part Two
The Journey

15: Dating Chaos

Chaos is a Ladder.
-   ***Lord Baelish, GOT***

A very difficult year passed. Kevin managed to get back on track and although money was still tight, we at least had an income again. I was in the process of setting up a stress management company and planned to offer stress management solutions to commercial banks in London. Having no clue about stress management myself, I was going to hire stress management practitioners to deliver courses to my new clients.

all I needed were said clients

Through my contacts, I managed to arrange some meetings, but was surprised when I was unable to secure any sales. I thought everyone would want this, but meeting after meeting resulted in nothing and I was amazed. My fantasy of becoming a successful, independent, businesswoman,

overnight

wasn't happening and I was raging.

Still living in the family home, sale after sale fell through and in the end it made more financial sense to keep it. Having already let go of it emotionally, I was happy to be staying but knew how volatile my world had become so remained detached. The kids were still in school, but only by the skin of their teeth and only because the school allowed us a payment plan, until we were financially secure again. My ring had paid the bulk of their fees but we still owed them money.

Kevin and I were drifting along as parents, busy doing our own thing. He was rebuilding his business and I was

very slowly

trying to build mine. It was tough and there were days when I wanted to throw in the towel but I kept going, hoping I'd get a break.

The romantic side of my life was non-existent but eventually I started dating again, met a few nice guys and had some fun, but my heart wasn't in it. One evening while on a date, I had an out of body experience that might have turned me off dating for life. I was having dinner with a guy: he was nice but I wasn't really into him. While we were eating, I became aware of someone talking.

Chat, chat, chat, chat, chat, who the hell is that?
Oh wait, it's me.

I sounded like a complete and utter maniac who clearly couldn't take a breath. Going on and on I was talking about myself the whole time and the poor guy sitting opposite couldn't get a word in. Needless to say, I didn't hear from him again.

After that, I felt strangely indifferent toward men. No one had my attention which in itself was unusual. More often than not I fancied someone even if it was just a crush, and I was feeling worried. Maybe I'd never feel interested in a man ever again. When I still felt this way a few months later, I began to question my sexuality. Sitting in my garden one afternoon, I read an article about a woman who'd left her husband for her best friend and was now extremely happy in her gay relationship.

OMG perhaps I'm a lesbian and
have been batting for the wrong team.

Unable to activate any desire for men, maybe I needed a woman. There were men asking me out, but I wasn't interested and felt dead inside. This article was proof that divorced men and women found happiness in gay relationships. Maybe that's what I needed to find my desire again.

My theory was tested sooner than I ever could have imagined.

A few weeks later I was out with a friend in London who introduced me to male friend of hers. He was gorgeous and I was instantly attracted to him. Finally, I thought, a spark and when I talked to him, I found him interesting as well. He invited me to lunch the following week, I said yes and was excited at the prospect of seeing him again. Not only because I fancied him, but because he was also an experienced businessman and said he'd help me with my business. My lack of success made me feel disheartened, deflated and disappointed so I'd take any help I could get.

Lunch turned into five hours of interesting conversation, lots of white wine and a little bit of flirting.

a lot of flirting on my part

A polite cough from the waiter alerted us to the fact that the restaurant was closed and they were waiting for us to finish. We laughed at how absorbed we'd been in each other as we made our way to the pub across the road and while paying for the drinks, he casually asked the barman if there was a quiet corner to sit in. 'I have a beautiful woman I want to kiss,' he said as he smiled at me.

I thought it was very romantic and of course let him kiss me, really hoping I'd feel something. Sadly there was nothing, not even a flicker and I was bitterly disappointed.

definitely a lesbian

After a couple of pints, we said goodbye, arranged another date and I jumped into a taxi to the train station, but on the way got a text from a girlfriend. She was in a bar close by and invited me to join her and some work colleagues for drinks. Now.... bear in mind, I'd spent the afternoon drinking white wine,

more than I could handle

I was absolutely in no condition to continue drinking and meet new people. I should have gone straight home.

but of course I didn't.

I went to the bar and drank even more wine and was soon introduced to a girl who was about ten years younger than me. She'd also been drinking quite a bit. She was very sweet and as we talked, I felt like she was flirting with me.

eh.. is she flirting with me?

I couldn't believe I'd just been thinking about my sexual orientation and this was happening. In all the years of going out to bars and clubs, I'd never been hit on by a woman until now, so in my inebriated state decided it would be a good opportunity to test my lesbian theory and began flirting back.

obviously a wise decision, in a bar full of
my friend's work colleagues

Before I knew it, we were kissing each other and I mean proper kissing, snogging in fact and quite explicitly.

mortified

On some level, I knew kissing her in a packed bar was not the place to test such a theory, but I was too drunk to care, so we continued kissing for what seemed like hours.

my inner lesbian was dancing a happy dance

It was nice. Her lips were soft but it didn't really feel any different from kissing the guy earlier that day and not a shred of desire was activated. Too much wine, no excitement, no desire and no interest, I went home.

alone

When I woke up the next morning, I was absolutely mortified. I couldn't believe that first, I'd gotten so drunk in front of people I'd never met before and second, I'd kissed two people on the same day. A man who I kinda liked and a woman who's name I didn't even know. My god, what was wrong with me?

During our morning dog walk, I told the girls and they laughed their asses off. I could see the funny side, but I also felt as if I was drowning in emotional confusion. I never saw the girl again and was quite sure I wasn't a lesbian, because in the cold light of day, I knew my attraction to the male was dominant and the idea of being intimate with a girl, unless I was smashed off my

130

face just wasn't for me, so with this in mind, I decided to see the guy again.

the first one I'd kissed that day

I thought maybe he could reawaken something in me and put the kissing experience down to the wine. We arranged to meet a few weeks later and began texting each other several times a day. When I started dating Kevin we had no mobile phones so this was very new to me.

flirty texting was pretty weird

On the evening of our date, I was delighted to find the conversation was still interesting. We picked up where we left off and although I wasn't really attracted to him, I convinced myself I was and went to bed with him. A complete and utter disaster. I was a wreck. Self-conscious and embarrassed, I focused only on how I looked and acted. What if he thinks I'm fat?

oh my God, I'm fat

Can he see my stretch marks?

he thinks I'm disgusting

What if I'm not doing this right? Am I moaning enough or maybe too little?

overthink, overthink, overthink.

It was a horror show and my overactive thoughts destroyed any chance of being remotely turned on. Of course, I pretended to have a good time and when we parted the next day, we made plans to see each other, but he immediately backed off and I felt sick.

what? you don't like me?

I was new to dating so immediately perceived his backing off as complete and utter rejection. I couldn't believe it and thought back on our night together, did he know I was faking? Then I thought about breakfast the next morning, he seemed keen and I was confused. Was there something wrong with me? Of course my self-loathing immediately kicked in; I was fat and ugly and a terrible lover who never shut up talking.

why did I not stop talking?

I'd been with my husband since I was 23 and now I was nearly 40. I didn't know how to do this and was unable to accept the fact that he just wasn't into me and I wasn't actually into him either. But I pursued him anyway. I'd text him casually and he'd respond to begin with, we'd flirt and that would appease my ego temporarily.

ok calm down, he likes you
you're not completely worthless

Deep down. I knew he didn't care, but I wouldn't accept it. I decided in my head we'd be great together, a great couple and I was going to make it happen. When I was getting nothing from him, I decided to shock him and texted him one morning to tell him I didn't think we were working out and we should finish it.

go Suzanne, girl power!

Imagine my mortification when a text came back saying he didn't know there was anything to finish, but ok and good luck. I read the text and wanted to die with embarrassment but it didn't stop me.

His offer of help with my business gave me the excuse I needed to keep in contact so I waited a few weeks and sent him an email.

stalker, I know.

We met for dinner and I spent the night with him, again it was mediocre but a pattern formed. We'd see each other every two months, we'd have dinner and spend the night together and each time I met him, I'd tell myself this was it, this was when our real relationship would begin. Of course it never happened and I was briefly aware of the feeling of *deja vu.*

sixteen and sitting at the Pope's Cross
in Dublin with my first boyfriend

I was in a cycle of negative behaviour, deluding myself but I didn't know it at the time. As time went on, he'd ignored my texts and there was absolutely nothing I could do about it. It was excruciating and the first time I'd ever experienced such a thing. I always answered his texts and couldn't believe it when he didn't answer mine.

Eventually though,

after about 18 months of bashing
myself against the rocks

I admitted defeat. I'd spent a day in London with him and finally realised I didn't actually like him. I'd become so focused on getting him, that I lost sight of that fact. I'd been trying to find ways to involve myself in his business to help him succeed and lost sight of my own success. The same thing I'd done with my husband, with my first boyfriend and any other man I was interested in. When I let him go, I had a renewed sense of enthusiasm about my own life.

My focus was back on me and my path to self realisation. I had a yearning to know more about myself and over the years had bought many self help books, but never read any of them. Now I wanted to read them, I wanted to self-develop, so instead of reading romance novels that left me feeling like I'd never find love, I began reading the self-help books I'd bought over the years. I knew something bigger existed and I wanted access to it. I knew happiness was an inside job, but I didn't know how to get to it.

Up until now I'd always believed it came from outside stuff, being in love, having loads of money, being successful and popular. Something about happiness being within resonated with me and I intuitively knew there was truth to it. I wanted this happiness that lived inside of me. If it was there, it was buried under years of fear and anxiety and I'd have to dig deep to find it.

16: The Law of Attraction

Thoughts become Things.
- *Mike Dooley*

Being on the path to self-realisation felt right. I knew I was supposed to be here and I was growing as a person. Enthusiastic about my study, my level of awareness began to increase but... I had no idea that facing my truth would be one of the hardest things I'd ever do. I was just basking in my new found spiritual direction and thought I had it all worked out.

I found the light

Reading and finishing books like *The Power of Now*, *The Alchemist* and *The Road Less Travelled* was completely new to me. In the past, I usually flicked through them, hoping something would jump off the pages and fix everything in my life. When that didn't happen by chapter three, I gave up and put the book down. Now I was reading them, no I was studying them and I couldn't get enough.

One day while running in the woods, determined to lose the extra 20 pounds I perceived to be the root of my misery,

I will be skinny!

my neck seized up. It had happened before, but never to this degree and I was in absolute agony as I made my way back to my car. It seemed whenever I got stressed or something bothered me, my neck hurt and lately I'd been stressed about making my business work, something that was proving impossible.

Why was I not a millionaire businesswoman by now?

Having already tried physiotherapy, acupuncture and massage, when a friend recommended an alternative kind of therapy, I decided to give it a go and the minute I met the therapist, I knew I'd done the right thing. I began seeing him on a weekly basis for neck massage and self-awareness discussions. His room was full of crystals, incense and books, lots of amazing spiritual books, and it was during one of our sessions that he recommended a book that broadened my perception more than ever before.

It was called Zero Limits. The story of the vibrational power of four phrases and how they could change your life. Until then, my level of awareness was based on having a positive mindset and although I knew there was something more, I didn't understand what it was. This book changed that, but it was the next book that really changed the game.

Mentioned in Zero Limits, I didn't pay too much attention, then I read about the same book in a magazine, then it was advertised on Facebook and then I saw someone reading it on the tube in London.

ffs read me Suzanne!

I'd never heard of it before and now it was everywhere. The book was presenting itself for me to read, which of course I did and nothing would ever be the same again.

It was called 'The Secret,' a popular and well known book about the law of attraction, something I'd never heard of before.

The Law of Attraction?

why had no one ever told me about it?

If I'd known such a thing existed, I was certain I'd have achieved much more in my life by now. It blew me away on every level. Like attracts like and thoughts become things. Events that happen in our lives are the direct result of our thoughts and emotions.

hang on, what?

Negative thoughts attract negative situations, worrying attracts more things to worry about and as a professional worrier, I could categorically confirm this. I began to see how I'd unwittingly created so much drama and chaos in my own life, because I was conditioned to think negatively.

eh....

The message was clear: where focus goes, energy flows. Like buying a red car, suddenly you see red cars everywhere, nothing changes except your focus. Most of my life was spent focusing on what I didn't want and surprise, surprise it kept turning up, because not wanting something, is still focusing on it. I always worried about money and over the years, we'd had it, lost it, had it, lost it again. I worried about never finding that ultimate feeling of love and of course, so far I hadn't. I worried about never finding success and all I'd experienced so far in my stress management business was stress. I was consistently getting what I didn't want because I consistently gave thought to what I didn't want.

someone shoot me now!

Learning about the Law of Attraction instantly resonated with me and made complete sense. I wanted to be in love, be successful and financially independent, have a great relationship with my kids and until now, I never thought any of that was possible for me. I thought I'd never find love, I constantly felt like a bad mother, and thought my business was bound to fail. I was sabotaging myself every step of the way and I didn't know I was doing it.

My focus was always on the negative. I worried about absolutely everything. If the kids got the flu, I convinced myself they had cancer. With a skin rash I'd envision them hooked up to a life support machine and a hospital referral had me seeing them in their coffins.

oh my God, they're going to die

Travelling with them was a nightmare as disaster scenes played in my mind. Hotel rooms had to be high above sea level

in-case of a tsunami

and if they were in kids clubs, they had to be checked on every half an hour.

in-case of abduction

Travelling without them was even worse. Every plane I stepped onto I imagined it plunging into the cold, dark sea, killing me and leaving them to grow up without me.

Having worried about money since I was a child, I lived with the notion that it was hard to come by. I had the mentality of lack and knew from my own childhood how difficult it was to be positive about money, when you had none. However, that was the secret; in times of challenge and when it seems impossible, shift your focus to the positive, visualise what you want, give thought only to that and trust in the Universe.

sounds easy.. right?

Instead of worrying about the kids getting sick, I should focus on their health. Planning escape routes while on holiday was utter madness. Worrying about money was futile, it was there or it wasn't and worrying did nothing to change that. If I wanted money, I had to focus on abundance, pay my bills with joy in my heart and believe in an abundant Universe that provides for everyone.

right, gotcha!

If I wanted love, I had to become love to attract it.

eh?

I had to fall in love with myself first.

how the fuck do I do that?

My success happened the same way, I had to focus on succeeding instead of always thinking I'd fail.

The book made it sound easy, but of course if it was, we'd all be multi-millionaires, married to our soulmates and wearing a size six. Knowing it is one thing, living it is quite something else. Having a positive mindset was actually easy, but maintaining it and really believing in it, was the tricky bit.

139

My positive thoughts were constantly being undermined by negative emotions.

much more powerful and easier to believe

My subconscious program ran on doubt and I second guessed myself at every turn. It only took a few seconds for any positivity I had to be drowned in a sea of negativity, but at least I knew this now. I knew what was going on and I was determined to understand it completely.

Devoting myself to it like a research project, I read every book I could find on The Law of Attraction. I needed to know everything about this subject and was astonished to discover that it was our emotions that stop us from getting what we want. We can trick ourselves into believing we're being positive, but we can't trick the Universe. It's the vibration we send out that is unmistakable. I was trying to be positive when my life fell apart, pretending, smiling and telling my friends and family that everything was ok, but inside, I was trembling in fear and attracting more reasons to feel that way. You can't think it will be ok and not feel it. The emotional connection makes it happen.

To get what you want, you have to be absolutely positive it's already on its way, with no doubt whatsoever. The emotional connection when projected out to the Universe, is attracted back. I got all that in my head, but I couldn't feel it and I desperately wanted to feel it.

please let me feel it

Soon though reading about it wasn't enough. I began watching spiritual teachers on YouTube. Stuart Wilde, Eckhart Tolle, Bob Proctor and Tony Robbins. I soon realised their message was the same, only delivered in a different way. People who had happiness, joy, love and abundance in their life, chose it. Consciously or subconsciously they chose it and simply didn't accept anything less. They expected the good in their lives, invited it and smiled when it turned up.

Until now, I lived my life with doubt, fear and uncertainty, but something deep within me obviously wanted more, because over the years I'd attracted abundance. I got my champagne lifestyle, I got the material life I desired, but because I felt like I didn't deserve it, I'd lost it time and time again. I invited a shitload of pain and uncertainty into my life and lived with a mentality of lack, lack of love, lack of money, lack of self-belief, lack of time, lack of energy and lack of appreciation.

I couldn't have been more negative if I tried

Discovering the Law of Attraction opened a door to the Universe and I couldn't believe what I'd been missing out on. I felt enthusiastic and excited, but I wanted more and not knowing the next step, I decided to ask the Universe for guidance and a few short weeks later when I was given a direct answer, I was flabbergasted.

17: Getting To Know Me

A journey of a thousand miles must begin with a single step.
   -   ***Lao Tzu***

Focus on the positive and be more present. Yep, I got that,

in my head

but I was still living in the clutches of anxiety. Having gained a tiny bit of self-awareness, I was better at talking myself out of unnecessary worrying. Most of the time I didn't even know what I was worrying about but had become so good at it, that I could worry about nothing for days.

I had a deep aversion to just being myself; the people pleaser in me could easily adapt to the people in my life, usually agreeing with them during conversations,

even if I disagreed

or putting myself out to please them and gain their approval, usually telling belittling tales about myself,

just to make them laugh

constantly self-deprecating, because I wanted them to like me. Now that I'd become aware of this, I found it exhausting. My friends would often tell me it was ok, just be myself, but 'be myself?'

ew! what a horrific thought!

142

That would mean being the real me, a woman in pain, a woman full of confusion and desperate for someone to love her. Nah. No one got to see that.

except me

When my marriage was failing, I opened up but very quickly closed down again. My deepest thoughts and feelings were firmly pushed to the furthest part of my mind

where they belonged

and on top of that, I was now unable to cry. In the past two years, my tears had dried up and no matter how hard I tried, watching sad movies or listening to sad songs, I just couldn't activate them.

great, more suppressed emotion

I knew it wasn't healthy but tried not to focus on it too much. Instead I slowly allowed this new version of me to emerge, trying to accept the changes in my life, rather than resisting them every step of the way. Having already asked the Universe for guidance going forward, I decided to ask Google as well. The Universe might take time but the answer from Google was immediate. I typed in self-awareness courses and it provided hundreds of them.

even more confusing and actually no help at all

I didn't know which one was worth my time or my money and while pondering it, something incredible happened.

the Universe said hold my beer

Out of the blue and I mean seriously out of the blue, I received an email from my cousin in Dublin. I hadn't seen him in years and in fact didn't really know him at all. I have hundreds of cousins in Ireland, some I'm close to and others, not at all. He was in the latter category and receiving an email from him was seriously random. He told me he'd gotten my email address from my mother with the intent of telling me about a spiritual organisation he was part of,

wait for it...

in London. He asked if I'd like more information and I sat staring at the screen thinking, is this for real?

When I recovered from astonishment, we had a couple of phone conversations and taking his recommendation, I booked myself onto a weekend course a month later and felt excited about it. This was me being guided by the Universe onto the path of self-discovery.

I was obviously special

It was also my first experience of being with people on a similar journey. Until now I'd been going through this completely alone, except for books and videos and I was absolutely gobsmacked when I turned up at registration and saw so many people going through the same thing.

what? I'm not the only person in the world going through an emotional meltdown

144

At first I was slightly miffed at my non-exclusivity, but also relieved as I realised these were people I could talk to, people who might have some answers.

The course consisted of four full days of personal development, quite brutal in some ways as it completely stripped you bare. The coaches encouraged complete honesty, claiming most people are dishonest about who they are with everyone, including themselves.

definitely me

At the end of the weekend, they promise to answer humanity's biggest question: What is the meaning of life?

It was harrowing at times, there were tears and tantrums. Watching people face their truth in a room full of strangers was an unforgettable experience. Thought provoking questions were asked and a fairly aggressive coaching style allowed some people to have amazing breakthroughs. I watched it all, fascinated at what I witnessed, but nothing happened for me. I was still deep in my chaos and felt quite envious of those getting life changing revelations.

where was mine?

As I looked around the room on the last day, I realised that when you're desperate for help, you look for it everywhere and we were all desperate. We listened to every word our coach said, hoping against hope that something he said would help free us from the pain of waking up and needing answers.

As in all the books, the message was the same, everything we need is within us, live in the present moment, be truthful no matter what and be authentic, dare to be yourself, take responsibility for your life, even if it hasn't turned out how you expected it to, stop glossing over everything, stop trying to convince yourself that you're happy and stop trying to fit in.

I'd never taken responsibility for anything. I put that onto someone else, then if I was unhappy, I could blame them.

yay, not my problem

I was terrified of being an authentic version of myself.

see the real me? no no no no no

I struggled to speak my truth and had always tried to fit in

do you like me? please like me,
what do I need to do for you to like me?

I didn't know I was supposed to stand out and be a true authentic version of myself. I didn't know how to do that, but at least I now knew, I didn't know.

conscious incompetence

Walking to the tube station at the end of a very intense weekend, I felt quite reflective. I understood what they said on an intellectual level, but I still couldn't live it. My fear held me prisoner and I felt disappointed that I'd been unable to let it go. I honestly believed I'd walk into the course on Thursday morning and walk out a different person on Sunday night, but I was still the same person. I knew a bit more about myself and the weekend had given me some answers, but with a sense of dread, I realised I'd only scratched the surface.

146

A few weeks later while dropping my son to school, I was surprised when I received another nudge from the Universe. During coffee with the mums, someone mentioned Tony Robbins and a seminar in London the following month. 'Unleash the Power Within.' Four days of high energy, high emotion, smash through your fears, take on the world kind of stuff. Exactly what I was looking for, so of course, I made enquiries and booked my place.

Spirituality can be expensive and money was still tight.
This was me, discovering who I was,
while plunging myself into debt.

I convinced three of my girlfriends they needed this in their lives and we arrived at the Excel Centre in London feeling optimistic and excited, until we walked through the door. Glancing nervously at each other, we thought we'd made a terrible mistake. The music was loud, every member of the crew was singing, dancing, jumping around and clapping their hands. High fives were being dished out and hugs were given to anyone who wanted one and that was just at registration. 'Good job,' was the phrase of the day and we were absolutely horrified. Completely over the top, American bullshit, we instantly regretted paying five hundred quid each for a ticket.

However, when we took our seats feeling deflated and self-conscious, Tony Robbins appeared on stage and literally within minutes, we were hooked. The man was mesmerising. The whole room fell under his spell and a rollercoaster of emotions followed for the weekend. We laughed, cried, walked across a path of fire,

an actual one

147

danced, sang, gave high fives to everyone we passed, hugged strangers and 'good job' became our new favourite phrase.

It was infectious and everything we dreaded on the way in, became everything we loved on the way out. Change your state of your mind and you can change your life. Wow. Was it really that simple? I got what he meant and the euphoria of the weekend was wonderful. Like riding the crest of a wave, we all felt exhilarated. It took about two weeks for my anxiety and despair to return, but I was more in control. I could practice changing my state and it was becoming easier to do so.

a titchy tiny bit easier

Many other weekend courses followed, some good, some not so good. I was still trying to figure out my life. How my marriage failed, if I drank too much, why I always seemed to be chasing after love and money and why nothing felt easy. My business was limping along but no matter how hard I tried, I couldn't seem to make a pound.

I mean how hard can it be?

Still, I was 100% committed to this world of self-awareness, it captivated me and I was determined to find answers and be a better version of myself, even though fear was still my overriding emotional state. I knew this fear wasn't real, I knew it was an illusion, but knowing that didn't make it go away. My instinct was to be afraid. It was deeply ingrained into who I was, but at least I could now observe it as it crept into my life and took over the decisions I made on a daily basis.

piss off fear

The voice in my head didn't want me on this journey; it's very existence was threatened by my increasing self-awareness. My thoughts would tell me that if I continued, I'd lose myself and be sorry. I'd lose my friends because no one would like this new version of me and I'd be alone, lonely and regret not sticking with what I had. However, instead of being terrified by these thoughts as I had been in the past, I could now watch them and was less affected.

still a bit, but less

I had evolved. I was better at changing my state. I knew how the law of attraction worked. I was practicing gratitude, writing down my thoughts and visualising my life as positive. I was reading everything with the word spiritual in it and I lived more and more in the present moment. I had knowledge, I had awareness, but I still had resistance. Only when I let that go would I experience real change.

18: Spiritual Awareness

Your own Self-Realisation is the greatest service you can render the world.
- ***Ramana Maharishi***

A few months later I was attending a business conference in London when the nudges I'd been receiving from the Universe turned into a hard push. It was a three day business seminar and I told myself

several times

it was good for networking, but I was actually bored out of my brain and spending money I didn't have. At this point I still confused movement with progress and thought that looking busy meant I was achieving something.

There were speakers from all over the world. Bill Clinton was one of them and they all spoke about business success and how to get it. It was very long and very boring and I was kicking myself for wasting more money. However, on the last afternoon, a panel of businessmen on the stage discussed leadership in business and one of them answered a question from a member of the audience. I can't remember his exact answer, but when he spoke I immediately stopped what I was doing,

checking my Facebook page

and listened to him. His mannerism and his use of language touched me in some way and I thought there was something very spiritual about him.

He spoke about the Universe and personal responsibility, telling the audience that when we take full responsibility for our life, it gets better, personally and professionally. The second I heard him referring to the Universe, I was captivated and listened intently to what he said. An hour later, when he came off the stage, close to where I was sitting, I hotfooted over to introduce myself. I asked if he spoke anywhere else. He said he did and taking my business card, said he'd be in touch. I really hoped I'd hear from him again.

A few months later I received an email and was surprised to discover he was a spiritual teacher at the Kabbalah centre in London. His email was to invite me to attend a course called, 'The Power of Kabbalah One.' Now, like most people on the planet, the only thing I knew about Kabbalah was that Madonna was into it, so I Googled and decided to go along to an introductory evening. I had no idea what to expect but went along with an open mind and as I listened to this man speak, everything he said made sense to me. I had a powerful need to explore it further so signed up for a course,

another one

and began studying it immediately.

Kabbalah teaches you to be proactive instead of reactive in your life, to listen to your soul instead of your ego and to receive the light of the creator with the intention of sharing it.

doesn't that sound like a nice way to live?
I thought so.

I already knew the voice in my head was referred to as my ego and when my teacher explained we were much more infinite

151

than that, I practically wept. Deep down I knew this and hearing it out loud was such a relief.

Hearing that it was our intuition and our soul that defined us, made me dizzy because although I'd read about it in hundreds of books, I'd never heard it explained this way. My higher self rejoiced as a piece of a puzzle I didn't know existed dropped into place. All the books and all the courses led to this and everything I'd ever read was being discussed in great detail, in a classroom full of people on the same journey. I felt like I'd come home.

I already knew I was personally responsible for my life and everything that happened in it, good and bad, but knowing that and fully accepting it are two completely different things.

How can I take responsibility
for all the shit I didn't want?

I was still unable to get past my fear and make real changes but Kabbalah would take me to the next level. I was interacting with likeminded people, getting answers from spiritual teachers who radiated internal peace and it allowed me more clarity and a deeper understanding of who I was.

My ego began to quieten and my anxiety reduced. I felt like Kabbalah was showing me the way and Thursday nights at the London centre became my favourite part of the week. The bookstore selling Kabbalah books was my new favourite place and each week I'd buy a new book to read on the train home. Shabbat on Friday night was a different world where I could pray and meditate with my new friends, then eat in celebration and gratitude.

shabbat shalom

I learned the things that truly matter in life are the things we can't hold in our hand. If we can't see it and only feel it, it's a true source of joy. Love, appreciation, gratitude, happiness, trust, honesty, integrity and so on. I learned about the bigger picture, about true purpose and how immediate gratification was the work of the ego. True fulfilment comes from resisting what we think makes us happy and allowing life to flow. Many of my childhood questions were answered and I loved being part of this community.

I discovered I'd been reactive all my life and I was a blamer, everything that went wrong in my life was always someone else's fault. Not having a career was my parent's fault.

they didn't force me to go to university

I was overweight because I didn't have time to eat properly or exercise.

obviously the kids' fault

I didn't have love in my life because I'd felt emotionally deprived as a child.

ahem... dad? anything to say?

My need for blame was absolute. It was reactive and irrational, but I didn't understand any of that until now. The proactive person responds to challenges in a thoughtful and calm manner. They take full responsibility for their life and blame no one.

Kabbalah was therapy for my soul, the weekly classes, monthly one to one sessions and Friday night Shabbat dinners began to change me. This environment suited me and after a few months, I felt more secure about my life than ever before. My anxiety was fading fast.

One night during class we did a very important guided meditation. I was too embarrassed to ask if I could sit closer to the teacher, afraid to admit that I couldn't hear him. People tend to dip their voice during guided meditation and although I could hear in normal circumstances, I had to watch the face and read the lips of the person speaking. Meditation meant my teacher was speaking quietly and my eyes were closed so I couldn't hear him.

When it was over, my classmates were overwhelmed by the significance of it, crying and hugging each other and I was devastated I missed it.

fuck!

I'd been actively ignoring the fact that my hearing had degenerated further. It had been five years since my last hearing test and I was unwilling to accept hearing loss on top of everything else in my life.

I am not going deaf

If I didn't hear a person talking to me, I got flustered and embarrassed. Sometimes I'd pretend to hear them, frantically trying to work out what they said, I'd smile or reply to what I thought they said.

it often sounded weird

I hated the thought of going deaf and felt as if I was less than other people and ashamed of yet another imperfection,

Suzanne the freak

but as I looked around my Kabbalah class in celebration, I knew I had to face it. I couldn't put it off another second. The next day, I booked an appointment at a hearing aid centre and wasn't at all surprised to hear my hearing had deteriorated further and I was almost 50% deaf in both ears. With my ex-husband's help, I bought hearing aids and when I walked into class the following week, I explained to my classmates that I was deaf, I was now wearing hearing aids and I could hear them properly.

suddenly my weird answers began to make sense

Having hearing aids changed my life. I couldn't believe what I'd been missing. The whole class celebrated in my acceptance of this and we all hugged and cried.

they cried, that still wasn't possible for me

I received a round of applause as they told me how proud and inspired by me they were and I was completely overwhelmed by it. I felt an appreciation, gratitude, harmony and love that took my breath away. I was in a room full of people who were open and unashamed about finding a deeper, more meaningful life.

The teaching of Kabbalah seeped into my soul. I finished the first course, and immediately signed up for The Power of Kabbalah two, then three. Each course went deeper into the teachings of the Zohar and I loved it. My relationship with my children improved and I found myself just wanting to be with them more.

Kabbalah allowed me to recognise the importance of my family and being a single mother to three lively boys was tough at times. I liked my time off, but now I was appreciating my children more each day and wanted to be around them. The boys noticed the change and at first thought it was weird when I tried to engage them more into one to one time, but they quickly got used to it and I felt closer to them.

One afternoon while at my monthly 'one to one' sessions with my spiritual teacher, we were trying to confront some past pain, process it and be free of it. When she recommended I seek forgiveness from my father for not being the daughter I should have been, I was gobsmacked.

wait, what?

Me seek forgiveness? Surely it was the other way round? He was never the father I wanted him to be and the reason I felt so unworthy of love and feeling quite self-righteous, I bloody well told her so.

'Do you think your father deliberately withheld his love from you?'

boom!

With that one question, I felt like I'd been punched in the stomach and immediately knew the answer was no. My father did not deliberately withhold his love from me, he just didn't know how to demonstrate it in the way I needed him to. That was okay for my brother and sister growing up, but I always needed more. That need was in me, not him and I was responsible for my feelings of emotional deprivation, not him.

holy fucking shit!!

The next time I flew to Dublin, I asked my father to forgive me for not being the daughter he wanted and even though my family thought it was super weird,

eh....

my dad gave me his forgiveness and I gave him mine.

for not being the father I thought he should have been

My relationship with him wasn't magically fixed, but it was lighter. I could see very clearly he'd done all he was capable of doing and was every bit a product of his childhood programming, as I was of mine.

By now my family thought I was wired to the moon and my mother honestly thought I joined a cult. I really tried not to preach but couldn't help myself.

hear ye, hear ye

I desperately wanted everyone to know what I'd discovered and what they were missing. I wanted to talk about the Universe, energy, self-development and spiritual growth, but people are not always in a place to make changes in their own lives. At the time it frustrated me, but it wasn't part of their journey. Self-awareness can't be forced. The desire to change has to come from within.

About two years after my first Kabbalah class, I stopped going. I don't know why, I just didn't need it anymore. I'd gotten so much from my time at the centre and it changed my life in an unimaginable way, but now I felt like the time had come to move on and grow in a different direction, one without a belief system perhaps?

My belief in the Universe was absolute, living in the present moment, being grateful, the law of attraction and the power of positive thinking had made my life so much better. I'd grown and developed, but my lack of purpose weighed heavily on my mind and I still felt desperately alone. Incapable of loving anyone in a romantic way, I really wanted to fall in love, but finding and falling in love with myself had to come first.

19: A Hint of Purpose

The meaning of life is to find your gift, the purpose of life is to give it away.

- *Pablo Picasso*

With my Kabbalah study complete, I was curious about other spiritual practices and began reading books about Buddhism and Hinduism. I was still looking for something but was unsure what it was. I liked what I read but didn't feel the need to go further and although I briefly considered Scientology, I changed my mind and decided to take a break from spiritual exploration for now.

lucky escape

There was part of me resisting something, but what was it?

an unconventional way of life

I'd been raised to fit in, but I was beginning to feel like I wasn't supposed to fit in and felt conflicted. Shaking off the belief that marriage, children, a steady job and so on were the keys to happiness was proving very difficult.

On the plus side, I felt more aligned with the Universe, I had spiritual realisation and a good amount of peace, but I lacked a sense of purpose. I really wanted to know what I was supposed to do with my life. I wanted to have a career and make some money instead of being financially dependent on my ex-husband. I had tried so hard to make my business work, but in three years I hadn't made a pound,

not even a penny

so I closed the company to focus on other things.

Around the same time, one of my girlfriends was going through marriage problems and although she had kept her feelings to herself for years, I knew her situation was bad and deliberately left her alone because having been through it myself, I knew she had to work it out on her own. When the day came for her to open up, it was like the bursting of a dam.

or an explosion of one

I knew I could help her. I knew how it felt to hide your feelings and suppress your emotions and I knew what happened when you finally let them go. I was still working through my own pain and even though I'd been through the mill, I was shocked by the force of hers. In my darkest hour, I didn't think I'd ever felt the despair and annihilation she was going through.

We'd walk the dogs every day. She'd talk about her life, how desperately unhappy she was, how her marriage was definitely over and how everything had to change. She'd make excuses, seek validation, look for approval, ask advice and try to work it out in her head. By the time we finished walking, she usually felt better. The next day, she'd change her mind, convince herself it was all in her head and there was nothing wrong.

okay then!

Every day was different. She'd cry about the wasted years and blame her husband, then she'd cry about the wasted years and blame herself and all I could do was listen while she tried to make sense of it all. As she hit rock bottom, I offered some insight and advice based on my own experience and tried to reassure her that rock bottom was a good place to be.

160

I told her pain was an excellent teacher, if we just learned from it, but of course in her panic and despair she found no comfort in this, even though she appreciated the help.

I worried about her state of mind but was also fascinated to watch it.

this chick was imploding right before my eyes

Until then I'd only ever experienced my own pain and watching her go through such misery, fear and suffering was intense. It catapulted me back to a time in my life when I went through the very same thing. Everything she said to me was everything I'd said to myself four years earlier. Her fear, uncertainty and devastation was my fear, uncertainty and devastation. I'd already walked this path and I suddenly realised how far I'd come.

Here I was in a very different place, the one giving answers, the one understanding and the one helping. Steven Covey said in his book, *The 7 Habits of Highly Effective People* that most people listen with the intent of responding, we don't listen properly because we're usually thinking of something good to say. For the first time in my life, I was listening.

actually listening

We spoke in the morning when we walked the dogs. She called most afternoons and sometimes when the kids were in bed at night. Her fear, panic, regret and guilt were tearing her apart. She apologised for taking up so much of my time, but I really didn't mind. Since shutting down my business, I had the time to talk to her and I smiled as I realised everything happens for a reason. The Universe had guided me to this, I was supposed to help her, because suddenly there it was…a hint of purpose.

Helping her was helping me and for the first time in my life, I felt fulfilled.

I made sure I was available to talk to her because I knew what this desperation felt like. I'd taken the hard path and fought through most of my pain on my own and as I helped her, I wondered if I could help others. Could I be a therapist? Was that my purpose? I didn't think so as going back to school for years was definitely not for me. I was a terrible student and had always been crap at studying.

massive crammer

As I thought about it however, the Universe clobbered me with the answer. I was having lunch with some girlfriends and one of them was talking about her husband's new job. She said how much he loved it and when I asked what he did, she replied, 'He's a life coach.' My coffee cup stopped before it touched my lips as I realised that was it, that's what I could be. A life coach. I suddenly recalled meeting one many years before on a TV program I'd been part of and thinking then, I'd like to be one, but had forgotten about it until that moment. Quickly finishing my lunch, I rushed home and immediately hit Google.

With a sense of urgency I hadn't felt before, I trolled through life coaching courses and when one in particular stood out, I gave them a call. After a long chat with the trainer, I booked myself onto the next available course and even though I knew doing a life coaching course didn't make me a life coach,

162

this course would give me the structure I needed. A platform to share what I'd already learned about being self realised.

A few weeks later on a rainy Saturday morning, I made my way to London for the first of five training weekends. Finally I would be something, I'd be a life coach. Unable to say that before, in the past if anyone asked what I did, I usually said, I was involved in this business or that. When this course was complete, I was a life coach who could help people, encourage self-awareness and promote positive change. This course would teach me how to do that and how to ask thought provoking questions instead of just giving my opinion.

something I was good at

There were about thirty other people on the course, some older, some younger and all trying to live a better life. The course content was great, it was interesting and I learned quite a lot about myself over the five weekend sessions. Spread out over a year, there was lots of reading and interactive learning in-between and about six months into the course, I got my first client.

little ole me had a client

At first, I followed the recommended method rigidly, but soon developed my own style. A more direct approach, I had a natural ability to make people feel at ease so got straight to the point. Of course I made my client aware of this at the beginning of our session and before I knew it I had two clients, then three. Finally I was doing something I liked and I was getting paid for it.

hooray!

Having chased after money for years, trying to make my business work, I didn't earn a penny. Now, I'd let it go, focused on what felt right and I was earning money.

kerching

Of course, at first I doubted myself and suffered with extreme imposter syndrome. What if my client asked a question I couldn't answer? What if I was exposed as a fraud, who knew nothing about self-awareness or life coaching. The voice in my head mocked me,

you're gonna fail, you're gonna fail

but I kept going. I kept learning life coaching techniques, expanding my knowledge and expanding my life. For the first time ever, I felt fulfilled and loved being able to say, 'I'm a life coach.'

I finally felt like I was getting somewhere in my professional life. Having spent years and years trying to figure it out, for the first time I was doing something that felt absolutely right. In my personal life, I was still somewhat emotionally shut down and remained distant and guarded when it came to my heart. I dreamed of falling in love, but I was afraid to let anyone in. It had been a couple of years since I'd even been on a date and although I knew longing for love pushed it further away, I still longed.

someone fall in love me...pleeeaaaasssseeee

164

I was trying to love myself more, but at this point I still believed everything in my life would be easier when I was wrapped in the arms of my lover. My problems would disappear and my life would magically transform into one of bliss, happiness and joy when my soulmate turned up.

a small expectation, no pressure on him at all

Helping other people with emotional problems helped me recognise some of my own and when one client went through huge emotional challenges while also in a loving relationship, I was confused.

what?

My belief that love conquered all was being challenged and I didn't like it. What could she possibly have to worry about when she was in love? Surely that was all that mattered. At first I didn't get it, but after a few months of helping others with similar situations, I was forced to consider the possibility that being in love didn't magically complete a person.

really? fuck...all my hopes were pinned on that

I had no choice but to consider the fact that romantic love was only part of the picture. Equally important was self-love, the love of family, the love of my children, my dog and of course, my life.

wow, get me! progress.

The only thing I could do was focus on being a better version of me. I was Suzanne the spiritual student, Suzanne the Life Coach,

Suzanne the mother and Suzanne the writer. Hopefully one day soon, I'd be Suzanne the lover.

20: Rejection, Rejection, Rejection

Be who you are and say what you feel,
because those who mind don't matter
and those who matter don't mind.
- ***Dr Seuss***

Ok, I got it, love didn't conquer all, but I still wanted a boyfriend so decided to at least try to open my heart, invite love into my life and be more lighthearted about it. Of course, as with everything I did, there were some serious teething problems to overcome.

It was August 2015 and my kids were in America with their dad. Sean was now 15, Ethan 12 and Sammie 10 years old. They'd adapted well to our way of life and we had a lot of fun together.

I was so proud of them

Kevin and I were divorced and quite good friends, we spent a lot of time together with the boys, often going on family holidays together or to dinner and a movie. The boy's biggest complaint was searching for a hoodie or a pair of trainers that were at dad's house while they were at mine and vice versa. It meant a lot of driving back and forth for me, but I thought it was the least I could do for putting them in this situation in the first place.

Sean was my rock who always made sure I was okay, and I adored him. He was talented, smart, kind and funny. Ethan was pre-teenage years and pushing boundaries.

hard

His recklessness terrified me, but apart from that, he was an amazing little boy. Sammie was always going to be my baby and was just adorable. Cute, smart and kind, everyone loved Sammie.

While they were away with their dad, I decided to go on holiday on my own.

I had no choice, my friends were busy with their families
and I had no fella

I booked a hotel in Lake Como for a week, then I planned to fly from Milan to Holland for a family party. Our finances were on the up and this was my first ever holiday alone. I thought it would be nice to reflect on my life, be present and just enjoy the down time. My meditation was strong, I was now practicing Transcendental Meditation every day and felt peaceful, energetic and happy. I was still lonely but refused to let it affect my life and having fantasised about Italy being incredibly romantic, I thought I'd find another piece of myself on this beautiful island.

and maybe meet a beautiful Italian millionaire
who'd sweep me off my feet
and fall madly in love with me

I fell in love with the lake, because how could I not? It was absolutely stunning and the hotel in Bellagio had views that took my breath away. Each day I woke up, meditated, had breakfast, studied, wrote, met new people, drank beautiful wine and generally connected with my higher self. I had a wonderful time, but I never felt more alone in my entire life.

get me out of here

168

The hotel was full of families and couples who were in love and I was alone on my sun lounger each day, alone having breakfast, alone for lunch, alone for the boat trips. A table for one at dinner every night became very tiresome.

The Italian man and the holiday romance thing truly only happen in books and being in this beautiful location merely emphasised my loneliness. Why could I not share it with someone special, the wonderful views and gorgeous Italian food and wine? It was a place for romance and I felt really alone.

bummer

Leaving Italy I felt rested but sad and was eager to get to Holland to see my family. It was my cousin Sharon's 50th birthday. The gang had arrived from Dublin and the party started. Having been there many times before, I always enjoyed Holland, but this time, I fell in love. Not with anyone in particular, just with Holland itself. I felt connected to the people and the energy of the country and found myself wishing I'd spent a week there, rather than laying on a sun lounger alone in Italy.

Following an amazing weekend, I was sad to leave, but my children were coming home soon and I was excited to see them.

A few days before the boys arrived, I met some friends in London for a drink and while there, bumped into a guy I used to date, briefly a couple of years before. We reconnected and chatted for a while and just before he left, he asked if I wanted to meet for lunch. I hadn't been interested the first time around, but I said yes. People change and maybe I was too picky.

here we go again

169

I hushed the voice in my head that told me I was wasting my time. I was trying to be open and that meant giving situations like this a chance. It was also a good opportunity for me to practice being emotionally vulnerable, something I'd already decided I needed to do.

Usually when I dated, I was ice cold and gave the impression that I was the strongest person on the planet who had her whole life figured out. Now I was trying to be a little softer, let the woman I really was peep out and be seen by others. A woman who was shit scared sometimes and just trying to get through life. Anyway I was tired of being alone and my week of being very alone in Italy was still fresh on my mind.

We went on a few dates, but after a few weeks he could tell I wasn't into it even though I tried to be. The chemistry just wasn't there. We agreed to end it, more his decision than mine. I might have dragged it out a bit longer, just to have someone over no one, but what happened next to my emotional state was astonishing.

Although confusing, it was also a huge emotional breakthrough and I'd soon realise why. As I said, I had no feelings for this man, none at all, but I felt as if my heart was broken and couldn't rid myself of the feeling of rejection.

no one is ever going to love me again

It made no sense. How could I feel rejected if I didn't want it? As with all of my emotional pain, it manifested in my stomach as anxiety and panic began to ravage me. Of course then my overthinking immediately kicked in.

there's something wrong with me.
I'll never have a relationship again

Then my insecurity kicked in.

he didn't like me and just wanted a way out
I'm too fat and I'm boring

Spiraling in a meltdown, I couldn't eat, couldn't sleep and convinced myself I was entirely to blame and could have made it work.

the fact that I didn't fancy him being totally irrelevant

A few tormented days later with extreme anxiety, no appetite and a few bottles of white wine, I actually cried. I was drinking with my sisters and felt so shit that I bawled my head off. It was drunk bawling, but crying was crying and I'd take it. It didn't help however as the next day I felt the same, just with an added hangover and I had to drive my son to rugby camp three hours away. Knowing I had to wait for him for five hours, I grabbed a book on my way out the door thinking I'd read for the afternoon.

As I dropped him off, I felt the need to be as far away from the other parents as possible. I was incapable of polite chat and barely holding it together so walked towards an empty field. Something was clutching me in a vice like grip and if I let go, I felt like I'd disappear into it. Squeezing from the inside, my chest was tight and my stomach muscles were flexed and unable to release.

The book in my hand was called 'The Untethered Soul' by Michael Singer, a book I'd read many times before and as I walked around the field, *in absolute agony*

I asked the Universe over and over to help me. Repeating in my head, thank you, thank you, thank you. I knew the benefit of expressing gratitude in difficult times and I wanted this pain gone. I didn't often have anxiety anymore and this attack was excruciating, so with vigor I continued my chant of thanks and was stunned when less than five minutes later I received the help I needed.

as in direct help from the source
knew I was special

The book fell out of my hand and when I reached down to pick it up, it opened at chapter six. 'The Secrets of the Spiritual Heart.' I'd already read this chapter and knew it was about releasing pain from your heart, but a very interesting thing happens when you read a self-help book. Reading it when you're in deep emotional pain, desperate for answers and reading it for self-improvement are two completely different experiences.

you pay more attention when you need the help

I remembered this chapter because I'd found it interesting before, but now I read as if my life depended on it. It said, 'pain is energy and if we don't process it, that energy builds up in our hearts.'

ok, got that, what's next?

It's called a Samscara. An energy impression on the heart that doesn't go away unless we process and clear it.

172

fuck, I had loads of them

I'd never processed any of my past pain, I just ignored it and hoped it would fade, which it did, but of course I didn't count on certain triggers activating it again. My current anxiety had nothing to do with some bloke rejecting me, it was years of rejection I'd ignored and this attack was the result of not processing any of it.

the straw that broke the camel's back

Everything I'd avoided and buried over the years had been building up on my heart and my body was screaming at me to confront and process at least some of it.

The method was to think of whatever was causing you pain, really think about it, allow it into your body and then just sit with it. Relax into it, breathe through it and ...smile. Smile or laugh because by doing this, you break the pain pattern. Smile, breathe, relax your heart and know you're releasing old pain. Don't push it back down, something I'd spent my whole life doing.

Astonished I was reading something so relevant to my current state of mind and with nothing to lose,

except hopefully the pain

I decided to give it a go. I thought about the pain in my life and knew I processed none of it. I always pushed it away, hoping it would sort itself out. The abortion I'd had all those years before and the grief I'd felt. The end of my marriage and the emotional chaos surrounding that. Never feeling good enough as a child, a wife, a mother. The pain of failure, the pain of feeling inadequate and the pain of disappointing people. Most of all the pain of rejection and abandonment I'd felt over the years and had just brushed it off.

I'd never given a thought to processing any of my pain. It was what it was and I just got on with it, but now I could clearly see why I was having a meltdown. I had a shitload of pain to work through, but first things first, the current pain of the rejection. I needed to sort this out because my body simply wouldn't function properly until I did.

ok, here goes

Taking a deep breath, I closed my eyes and allowed myself to feel the pain. I let it flow through me, taking note of the stomach ache and trying to relax into it. Slowly breathing in and out for about 15 minutes, I was smiling the whole time, horribly self-conscious and glad of the empty field.

I looked very weird

Repeating the process, my eyes closed, a smile on my face, I breathed in the pain and breathed it out again and just as I was about to give up, something happened.

ohh!

The tight coil of anxiety in my stomach loosened and I began to feel slightly better. So with renewed urgency, I kept going and holy crap it started to work. My anxiety loosened and before I knew it, I was really smiling, then I was laughing. The more I did it, the more relief I felt until the pain disappeared completely and I was laughing out loud.

Like the flick of a switch it was gone, released from my body and I could breathe again. The relief I felt made me want to dance but I kept walking, kept smiling and kept repeating thank you in my head. I knew I still had a lot of work to do and years of rejection to plough through but for now I felt amazing.

The rejection of my ex-husband, my 16 year old boyfriend, my father, friends, relatives and anyone else I'd unknowingly allowed to make me feel unworthy over the years would have to wait. That stuff was buried deep and wouldn't just magically disappear, but at least I knew I could work though it and I had hope.

When my son finished training he couldn't believe the transformation. On the drive there, I could barely speak and he knew the reason why. When he saw me he assumed a reunion had happened, but when I explained it was something far better, he was amazed. He had a good level of self-awareness at 15, because he had no choice. The Universe was my favourite subject and teaching my sons about it was my biggest priority. On the drive home, I described how it felt to release pain and was excited at the idea of releasing more of it.

I began to wonder why I'd put myself through so much shit. It took half an hour walking around a field in Oxfordshire to free myself of excruciating anxiety and I felt like I'd discovered a secret. In the coming months I'd use this method regularly when walking the dog in the woods, having a bath, in the shower or simply sitting in the garden.

process pain, process pain, process pain

Years of pain began floating away and I felt great, but some pain is buried deep, pain we are often unaware of until something triggers it. I had some digging to do to get to my pain, but if I'd known the depths I'd have to go to finally be free of it, I might have left it alone.

21: Trying to Love Me

There is no truth. There is only perception.
-   ***Gustave Flaubert***

Processing old pain set me free in many ways and gave me a new perspective on life. My heart was opening more, which was strange at first but I was optimistic and determined to be more lighthearted and have some fun.

I was sick of being so deep about everything

When my sister suggested a dating app, I thought why not and decided to give it a go. It was like shopping for men and I met a couple of interesting guys, nothing mind-blowing but I was out there again and enjoying it.

I still dreamt of falling in love, but what I wanted from a partner had now changed. Before my 'awakening,' I always thought my man would have a good job, a nice car, a decent amount of ambition and the desire for the finer things in life. Now I found myself dreaming about great conversation, amazing intimacy, deep connection, heartfelt friendship, respect, trust and of course unconditional love. Everything my Kabbalah teacher had talked about, the things you can't hold in your hand being what mattered most in life.

I was finally getting it

When my old neck injury flared up one morning, I was actually really surprised. I was releasing stuff and feeling connected to the Universe so WTF?

why strike me down like this?

I tried releasing it through relaxation and breathing, but when it turned into full blown sciatica, the worst physical pain I'd ever experienced in my life, I felt so let down and was miserable. From the left side of my neck, it travelled into my leg and I was in agony, limping quite badly for about six weeks.

It happened around Christmas time which meant I drowned my misery in wine,

even on the very strong medication

stuffed my face with comfort food and of course gained a shit load of weight. January saw me standing in front of a lady who ran the local slimming club. My sciatica had eased, but in two months I hadn't done any form of exercise and felt like a stuffed pig.

oink, onik

Sitting in the town hall, full of women mainly, I listened to story after story about food diaries, substituting fruit for chocolate,

which is completely unreasonable
and totally impossible

low fat cake recipes and counting steps, when an out of body experience occurred. I suddenly knew with absolute certainty this was not the solution for me, I simply had to find another way. At the end of the meeting, I still bought all the cookbooks and all the bars that had the promise of making me skinny and I left, but something had changed.

Three days later when on the phone to my mother in Ireland, something else happened. It was a month before her and my father's joint 70th birthday party and she said something she'd probably said a hundred times over the years. 'I want to lose a few pounds for my party.' It took a moment to hit, but suddenly I had amazing clarity and knew I couldn't do this anymore. I was 44 years old, my mother was 69 and she was still talking about losing weight. That was almost another 30 years and I couldn't do this for another 30 seconds.

no more!

The out of body experience from a few days earlier became clear and I knew in that second I had to make peace with my body. My issues had nothing to do with my weight, they had everything to do with my state of mind and if I didn't change that, I'd always perceive myself as fat. My need for perfection was absolute and if I didn't live up to what I believed my body should look like, I disgusted myself.

a smaller waist, a tighter ass, longer legs,
smaller shoulders, toned arms
anything else? oh and perhaps a facelift?

The question was how did I change years of yo-yo dieting and rid myself of deep rooted self-loathing? How did I release an impression on my heart so ingrained, that hating my physical appearance had become second nature to me?

I thought about the countless holidays and weekends away, ruined because I thought I was fat. A weekend away could turn into a nightmare because I felt so uncomfortable with my body, often buying two or three of the same things to wear. Usually something black and stretchy as I was always waiting until I 'got skinny,' to be more adventurous in my choice of clothing.

it never happened

During my marriage when we went on holiday with other couples, it was horrible. The other wives would look glamorous and beautiful and I'd be under enormous pressure to look good. I usually pulled it off, finding something cute to wear, but found shopping so stressful. I was never more than a stone overweight, twenty pounds at most, but I hated myself so much for not being perfect, that I usually got drunk to hide from the shame and humiliation of being

in my mind

the fat girl, in the same dress, night after night.

The conversation with my mother made me realise I always focused on what worked for other people and not for me. If someone got skinny through running, I'd run. If they did Weight Watchers, I'd do that. If they were in the gym or swimming, hiking or biking, I'd do all these things thinking if it worked for them, it would work for me.

it didn't

I hated running but all my runner friends were skinny, so I pounded the streets trying to be like them.

While processing all this, I went on a date with a French guy I'd met online. Even though I didn't want to go, my energy was negative and I was hungover, I said I'd go. So I went.

180

I was trying to live more by my word
and only saying yes if I was committed

I met him at the National Gallery in London and as I stood by the lobby waiting, I seriously regretted my decision to come. I was in the grip of a self-loathing attack and when he walked in and saw me, for a split second there was a look of disappointment on his face, which he quickly hid. But I had noticed.

We walked around the gallery together,

at hyper speed

both having mentally checked out. When we left to go our separate ways, I could feel my self-loathing gain momentum. It was building up to destroy me but this time I said no. As I walked down The Strand, I noticed my reflection in a shop window and I stopped to look at myself.

as in really looked at myself,
in my nice jeans and
blazer that looked really good

For the first time in my life I realised I'd been battering this woman for years, putting her through the ringer for how she looked and she didn't deserve it.

and I didn't actually look bad!

For as long as I could remember I'd been my biggest critic and I didn't want to be that anymore. On the train ride home, I let the rejection and self-loathing seep through me, no longer fighting it. I welcomed it with open arms and smiled. I smiled all the way home, noticing the beautiful countryside rolling by and focusing on the beautiful day it was outside.

I realised the most beautiful person in a room can be invisible if their energy is flat and a person not as physically beautiful can captivate a room by projecting a positive aura. My energy was determined on whether I felt fat or skinny. If I gained weight, was bloated, hungover or premenstrual, my energy was flat and I projected that into the world.

If I was feeling good and that might only be the result of a few days of eating well and not drinking alcohol, I felt amazing and my energy was elevated. Of course the French guy didn't like me, I didn't like me. My energy was chaotic and full of self-loathing, not the best receipt for what was technically a blind date. However, I immediately let it go. I wasn't overthinking that shit anymore and I certainly wasn't allowing it to block my newly opened heart.

no way, not happening

In my yoga class a week later I told my yoga teacher Terri about my quest to change my state of mind, rather than my body and she asked me two very simple questions, "What works for you Suzanne and how can you have the best version of your body?" It really made me think. Ok I was a bit curvy, but who says only being skinny is beautiful. Curvy girls can be beautiful too. Right? I did something that day that I'd never done before. I looked and I mean really looked at the other girls in my yoga class. There were some skinny girls, but there were curvy girls as well and as I looked at them I thought, 'what's not attractive about that?'

they were hot stuff!!

Each person had a different shape but still looked gorgeous, I saw the person I knew and not what type of body they had, and it hit me square between the eyes. I wasn't seeing my body, I had a mental image of my body that was distorted and people weren't as interested in how I looked as I thought they were. Was it possible that my body wasn't that bad after all and my curves were sexy?

hell yeah!

Thinking more on what Terri said, I asked myself what worked for me? What did I like? How did I like to eat and what exercise did I actually enjoy doing? That bit was easy, I loved hot yoga, it was my sanity. I could go there for an hour, switch off and concentrate on just being. It was my meditation through movement. What if I just did that? What if I gave up everything else and just did yoga?

Namaste

As for my diet! I could categorically state at this point in my life I had done every diet on the planet. I'd try it and usually lose weight but ALWAYS pile it back on. So what could I do differently this time? I knew I was never hungry in the morning, the thought of putting food in my mouth when I woke up made me feel sick and I also didn't like eating too late in the evening. If I imposed restrictions on calories or food groups, I lasted a week before binging to the point of feeling sick. So where did that leave me?

Intermittent Fasting. I'd read the books and I'd done it before, but the restriction of 500 calories on the two fasting days got me every time. Was there an alternative? I Googled it and came across something that might actually work for me. A daily 16 to 18 hour fast as a way of life. You finish eating at 6pm or 7pm and didn't eat again before noon the next day. I could easily do that. If you had a late meal or a night out, no stress, you just continued the next day or the day after that.

With this in mind, I cancelled my gym membership and decided then and there that I was a fasting yogi. I was only doing yoga from now on and I was going to fast as much as I could. If I had a crazy weekend, I'd go back to yoga on Monday and continue my fasting. I wouldn't throw in the towel and binge for two weeks like I normally did.

nom, nom, nom

Within weeks something happened. I felt different. I liked just being a yogi and found fasting worked for me. When I went to Vancouver with a girlfriend a few weeks later, instead of dreading it because I wasn't skinny, I bought some new clothes and made sure I had something nice to wear each day that fit my curves.

there, that wasn't so hard, was it?

For the first time, I really enjoyed a weekend away without thinking about how fat I looked. I was still curvy, but the negative energy was gone. I was rocking my curves, loving myself and ironically was bombarded with male attention for the whole weekend.

Coco Channel said, "Beauty begins the moment you decide to be yourself." The guys in Canada were all over me because I was loving myself.

184

When I got back to the UK, I went back to yoga, started fasting again and my body started to change. I became more interested in what I was eating in my six/eight hour eating window and made sure my food was healthy and nutritious, not always, but most of the time. Before I knew it, I'd lost 20lbs and I wasn't even trying.

This was the first time in my life that I had consistency with my diet and it was down to finally giving myself a break and making peace with my body.

22: My True Purpose

The soul is the truth of who we are.
- *Marianne Williamson*

Even though the voice in my head still tried to tear me down, I was better at ignoring it and was loving myself more. I focused only on what I wanted from my life and knew that no matter what, the voice in my head would always be there and my response to it would determine how I lived.

For the first time in my life, I actually liked myself,

finally!

I was slimmer, fitter and no longer postponing my life because I felt fat. Instead of projecting it into the future, telling myself when I got skinny, I'd do this or I'd buy that, I lived in the moment. With a spring in my step and a shiny new perspective, I marched forward.

Forward, march

Meditating every day, I was also writing, life coaching, hanging out with my kids more and just generally enjoying my life. As a mother to three boys, we were a rugby family so I spent a lot of my time on the side of a rugby pitch screaming and shouting. It was great fun and I now loved it.

On occasion my anxiety flared, usually the result of drinking too much alcohol but instead of being incapacitated by it, I now knew it was temporary and could observe as it crept through my body, attached itself to my stomach in a vice like grip and squeezed. I'd simply breathe my way through it trying to send loving energy to it, gently releasing myself from its grip. It wasn't easy but it wasn't as hard as it used to be.

progress

I discovered my body was programmed to experience anxiety. It was genetically encoded into who I was and I had to retrain myself. I had to re-learn how to relax by telling myself I was safe.

I'd felt unsafe my whole life

I'd do short meditations using powerful affirmations and repeating phrases like, 'I'm safe,' 'I'm loved' and 'I'm happy.' This really helped and before long, I began to feel that way.

Alcohol was a negative aspect of my life and the after effects could emotionally destroy me for days. I suffered more than anyone else I knew and I had a theory about that. I surmised that because I did a lot of meditation, I was on an elevated frequency and full of positive energy. Therefore, hangovers affected me more as being in said elevated state meant I had further to fall with a hangover and higher to climb to get back on track.

Socrates Suzanne - An unexamined life is not worth living

However, even though I knew this, it didn't stop me from drinking and on my child free weekends, I spent most of my time in a pub.

Apart from that, I felt great. I was aligned with the Universe and felt connected to everything. If I thought about someone, they appeared in front of me. If there was a particular song in my head, it would come on the radio. Parking spaces jumped at me, *my own parking god especially assigned to find me a space*

and my general attitude towards life had improved. Without anxiety and self-loathing constantly hanging around my neck, I was seeing the beauty in my life, because I was now looking for it.

My focus was on the good instead of the bad and of course where focus goes, energy flows. I kept getting more. I loved being a life coach, helping people figure out their own journey, I was writing more, I had a level of peace that was new to me and even though romantic love was still missing, I didn't yearn for it as much as I had in the past. I knew it would come when it was supposed to.

At a trampoline park with my sons and my nephew one Sunday evening, I bumped into a group of friends who were also there with their children. I hadn't seen them for quite some time, so sat down to have a cup of tea and a chat. Feeling energetic, positive, and peaceful and they noticed the change. I was talking about self-awareness, my favourite subject and how it transformed my life, when one of the girls asked if I gave any talks on the subject.

what? talks on the subject?

My interest immediately spiked and I heard myself saying, 'Yes, I do, I'm going to be giving one very soon.'

wtf?

I had no plans to do any such thing, but her question touched something in me and I knew I wanted to talk about this. I decided

188

to wing it by telling them I'd let them know when my next talk was and just before I left, one of them asked for my help preparing a nutritional presentation she was delivering to a large insurance company in London the following week. I of course said yes.

A couple of days later she arrived at my house and we worked on her presentation together. As a thank you, she said she'd give my details to her contact in the City and ask if I could give one of my talks on self-awareness. Right there in that moment I knew, without doubt that I was going to be a professional speaker.

boom!

It hit me hard as I realised it was something I'd wanted for a very long time, but was afraid to admit or tell anyone in case I looked stupid. As I looked at this woman who was about to go and speak in London without any fear of ridicule from others, any resistance I had melted away and I no longer cared. I wanted to be a speaker. I wanted to tell people about this incredible journey of self-realisation I'd been on, to share what I'd learned about myself along the way and hopefully help anyone going through the same thing.

I knew I had a voice that people listened to and had always been able to hold a room. I'd read thousands of self-awareness books and done more courses on self-realisation than I could count. I knew how to access the best part of me and I wanted to show others how to do the same. Life coaching allowed me to help people on a one to one basis, but I wanted to do it on a bigger scale. I wanted to inspire those who didn't even know a journey existed and guide them toward a path of self realisation.

189

The whole time I'd been afraid of what people thought about me,

Suzanne declaring her dreams to the world

the deep rooted people pleaser terrified of their reaction. Suddenly none of that mattered and I wasn't scared anymore. I wanted to be a speaker, I knew it was part of my purpose in life and I was finally ready.

A couple of years earlier, I had attended a public speaking university, my instinct for speaking already active, but I was disillusioned by a sales oriented environment. Spending four days in a London hotel, I did learn how to become a speaker and how to pitch myself in a very competitive market, but it was very daunting. I liked the speaking side of it, being on the stage and looking out at a room full of people. That thrilled me and I knew I did it well because so many people

also on the course

approached me that weekend to tell me they thought I was a great speaker. However, at the time, I still didn't believe in myself and I didn't know how to make it happen, so subconsciously put obstacles in my way. I told myself that getting into the business of speaking was tricky. I wasn't famous, I had no book published

yet

and I had no subject. What would I talk about?

Now I had a subject. I was a divorced mother of three boys who had been on an incredible journey of self-realisation and I wanted to share that. Instead of looking for obstacles, I decided

190

to open up and allow the Universe to decide as it had many times before and just like that, it did. Two weeks after my declaration, I received an email from the same insurance company in London, inviting me to talk to their employees about self-awareness. As promised, my friend had given them my details and I had my first paid speaking job booked.

oh my god!

Even though I was a nervous wreck, it felt right. I was a speaker, of course I was a speaker. I thought back to the many black tie events I'd attended over the years and how envious I'd felt of the guest speakers. I wanted to be on the stage and now I finally had a chance to make that happen.

For weeks I worked hard on my presentation, determined to deliver a message that inspired self-awareness in my audience.

I was shitting myself at the thought of not doing so

I wanted to capture their attention, reach out to those who felt discontented, displaced or had the feeling something was missing from their lives and let them know there were answers. That an amazing journey existed and it was one that could transform their lives forever.

When the day arrived for the talk, I made my way to London and finally stood at the top of a room with more than one hundred people waiting for me to inspire them, and I wanted to throw up.

what the fuck have I gotten myself into?

Adrenaline pumped through my body and at one point I honestly thought I was about to faint, but as soon as I started talking, I lit up

like a Christmas tree.

and gave an hour-long presentation called, 'Being The Best Version of You.' Afterwards there was a line of people waiting to talk to me.

me! they were waiting to talk to little ol' me

Some asked for my help with their emotional state, others had questions about the books I recommended and when one lady said I spoke to her soul and she felt like I was in her head, I wanted to cry. It meant so much to me and I'd never felt more fulfilled in my life.

My first talk was done and dusted, and I was paid for it.

five hundred and fifty smackeroonies

After that, the floodgates opened and I was no longer afraid. I wanted to tell everyone I met that I was a professional speaker and it felt incredible. Looking stupid in front of other people had forced me to hide my true desire. Comments like, 'who does she think she is,' or 'what has she got to offer,' were my biggest fear, but it didn't scare me anymore.

whoop woo

I felt like I'd looked it in the eye and wanted to shout out loud that I was a speaker. I have always loved the sound of my own voice, I'm also Irish and a natural storyteller.

this was definitely the right job for me.

If I failed, who cared? At least I gave it a shot and anyway, I had another theory about being able to speak so easily.

philosopher Suzanne again

Public speaking remains the one thing the majority of people feared most after death. I absolutely loved it and I knew I was good at it, so my theory was this: I was now 50% deaf, completely dependent on hearing aids and believed my speaking voice was a consolation prize from the Universe. People listened to me and during my hour-long talk in the City, you could hear a pin drop. I had their complete attention and, in my opinion, that was a gift and I wasn't going to waste it.

I'd spent years searching for my purpose and, ironically, speaking about finding my purpose became my purpose.

in the words of Alanis Morissette:
isn't it ironic, don't you think?

I declared to all my friends and family that I was a Speaker and I wanted to talk about self-awareness. The Universe had guided me to it and it felt right. I was deeply connected, I was enthusiastic, passionate and determined to change the world with my talks about self-realisation. I could actually help people become more self-realised which in turn would create a better world.

I was obviously chosen for this

If I'd been as self-realised as I thought I was, I'd have known my tricky ego was still somewhat in the driving seat. Yes, I was a Speaker and that realisation was a huge breakthrough, but the idea of being in the spotlight motivated me more than any message I was trying to deliver. If I'd been deeply honest with myself, I would have admitted that my dream of speaking all over the world was based more on gaining fame and fortune, than spreading the light of consciousness.

but it was okay, I had to start somewhere

I was excited about finally finding my path, but I didn't know my soul still had some work to do. Tricked into believing I had it all figured out, I got cocky. I was enlightened after all, superior in my knowledge of all things spiritual and nothing negative would dare touch me again. I was happy, content. I saw the good in my life, instead of the bad and I felt at peace.

surely I had it all wrapped up?

I forgot that all emotions are temporary and the journey is ongoing. There was a huge lesson I still had to learn. A lesson about love that would be the hardest lesson of my life and if I'd known it was coming, I'd have run, faster than a bat out of hell.

23: Unexpected Love

I wanna wake up every morning to your sweet face.
-   **Shania Twain**

A few weeks before my first talk in London, I had met a man who would change my life forever.

I was in Brighton with my girlfriends on a sunny Saturday in June. Having spent weeks preparing my talk, a day out with the girls was just what I needed. I'd fully accepted romantic love was missing from my life but was trying to focus on the positive. The Universe had shown me my purpose and this distracted me from dwelling on the fact that I was still single. Falling in love no longer seemed to be the pinnacle of my life.

yeehaa, I had a world to change

I could now see how much love I already had in my life. I loved my sons and they loved me. I loved my family and friends, my dog, my home, my body and so much more. I finally understood what the spiritual teachers meant when they said, 'to attract love, you had to become love' and I felt like that was happening to me. I was becoming love, because I was seeing love everywhere in my life.

Of course I still wanted 'the one,' but hoped it would happen eventually and stopped longing for it.

not quite, but more than usual

My closest friends, Catherine and Kate were helping me celebrate how far I'd come on my journey, my mini success as a Speaker and the fact that I no longer needed a man to make me happy. "You wait," Catherine said, "you'll probably meet the man of your dreams tonight" and we laughed.

oh how we laughed

Following a raucous pub-crawl through wine bars, gay bars and all the bars in between, we found ourselves in a nightclub and while dancing the night away, I happened to look at the front door. As I did, two men walked in and I immediately knew I was going to talk to them. At first I thought they were French, but they turned out to be Dutch and as they made their way to the bar, close to where I was standing, I said hello and introduced myself.

pissed and full of bravado

We chatted for a while, then they went upstairs and I went back to dancing with my friends. However less than ten minutes later they were back and I'm not exactly sure how it happened, being slightly intoxicated,

hammered

but I was talking to one of them and next minute, I was kissing him. Oh what a kiss it was. I'd only been kissed by one other man like that and I'd married him.

My Dutchman and I spent the rest of the night talking and kissing, ignoring everyone else in the bar and getting to know each other.

sound familiar?
Dublin on a freezing cold night
in January many years before

196

When the time came to go our separate ways, we didn't want to leave each other but finally at 3am, he put his number into my phone, said goodbye and left with his friend. The next morning I woke up missing him and I didn't know why.

We began frantically texting each other and were desperate to see each other again but I didn't know if that was possible. He was visiting the UK on his motorbike for a week, touring the south coast and a few days after our night in Brighton, he asked me to meet him in Bournemouth which of course I did.

wild horses couldn't have stopped me

I was delirious with excitement and couldn't wait to see him. When I walked into the lobby of his hotel, he was sitting at the bar watching me and as I walked towards him, my legs felt like jelly. He stood up and immediately kissed me as he had on the first night and I knew this man was going to be very significant to my life.

He took me out to dinner, stopped in the middle of the street to dance with me and introduced me to the people we met as his wife. The most intimate night of my 44 years followed. The connection and attraction I felt for him was off the scale. Over breakfast the next morning, I was already half in love with him. He sat opposite and cried as he told me how overwhelmed he was by his feelings for me. He said I'd changed his life forever and he couldn't believe we'd found each other.

wow, was this for real?

I was completely swept off my feet by romance, although when we said goodbye I didn't know if I'd ever see him again. I lived in the UK with my children and he had a business and a life in Holland. I tried to keep it together and told myself he'd be in my life if he was supposed to be, but I wanted it badly. Three weeks later when he asked me to meet him in Bruges for the weekend, I was beside myself with excitement. I booked the Eurotunnel, had an emergency wax, coloured my roots and counted down the seconds until I saw him again.

When I got to Folkstone a few days later however, all trains to France were cancelled and I almost cried.

almost! crying still wasn't possible and apart from a drunken bawl with my sisters, it was over three years since I'd shed a proper tear

I was about to head home until a lightbulb moment saw me driving towards Dover, where I immediately boarded a ferry to Dunkirk and arrived in Bruges, four hours later than planned. When he walked out of the hotel to meet me, I hesitated at first and felt a little unsure, he wasn't what I remembered but when he kissed me, it felt nice so I pushed my uncertainty away and dove in.

If I'd paid attention, I might have noticed the Universe was making it hard for me, but of course I ignored the signs and enjoyed a weekend of love, the most beautiful and intimate weekend. We talked and laughed, we wandered through this beautiful city, holding hands and stopping every five minutes to kiss each other. Intimate dinners were followed by nights of passion and by the end of it I was fully in love with him. I'd finally found my soulmate.

When he dropped the bombshell about having a girlfriend, it didn't concern me.

198

well it did, but I glossed over it

He told me the relationship had been over for almost a year and he just hadn't made the break. Now he'd met me, he would and I believed him because how could I not? Nothing was as strong as our connection, no one on the planet had ever experienced love like this and we were the luckiest two people alive to have found each other.

I was naive, what can I say

Before I met him, I had a rule number one: no wife, no girlfriend or no interest, and I didn't break that rule. I wanted a man of integrity, one with honour and humility. Not someone already in a relationship who wanted a quick fling. I told myself I'd finally found true love with my Dutchman because this was the real thing. The rules didn't apply.

while completely overlooking the fact
that he was lying to his current girlfriend
to be with me that weekend

When we left Bruges however, my anxiety began to flare, even though he reassured me he was going to end his relationship so we could be together. This was it. We were in love and he wanted to live his life with me. There was no going back and I was over the moon. Yet, a few days later he texted to say he thought it would be better to do it after his holiday, that was already booked

with his girlfriend

and I was devastated. I had no choice but to accept it as I was off to South Africa on a rugby tour with my sons for three weeks. When I got back, he was going to Sri Lanka for another three weeks

with his girlfriend

and I was nervous, but once again he reassured me that all was okay. I was the love of his life and he was currently in a brother/sister type relationship that would end as soon as he returned from his holiday.

he just didn't mention they were still having sex

He constantly told me we were soulmates who would be together forever so I believed him.

sucker!

We talked regularly over the six weeks we were both away. When we got home, I waited everyday for a message to tell me his relationship was over. I was in agony, but he reassured me

again

it was happening very soon and I clung to that like a lifeline. I told him I couldn't have an affair with him, it had to be all or nothing and I meant it. Even if it killed me, I'd walk away as I couldn't share him with anyone else.

A few weeks later and three months after meeting him, he called me to say the relationship was over, he told her and it was done.

actually she read his texts and

He flew to the UK, told me he loved me and we could finally be together. It was one of the happiest moments of my life. I ignored the feeling of unease. I told myself he'd been unhappy in his relationship when he met me, now he loved me, I was the one and relationships break up every day.

piss off conscience

Walking through London one weekend, we held hands, took photos and constantly kissed each other. He'd told me a thousand times how much he loved me and for the first time in my life, I felt it. I felt totally and completely loved. This was what I'd searched for. This was what true love felt like and I was beside myself with happiness.

someone pinch me please

If he wasn't in the UK, we talked on FaceTime, our conversations deep and meaningful. He was new to self-awareness and we discussed the books he was reading and his thoughts on waking up to find himself on a spiritual path. We had a list of cities to visit together and planned trips to Rome, Dublin and an ice hotel in Finland. When I wasn't wrapped in his arms, I longed to be there.

As the months went on, he was so proud of me for writing this book and getting more speaking jobs. He was full of encouragement and love and it felt so good to have the support of my partner. I was so sure he was my prize from the Universe. I was such a dedicated student, conscious and self-aware in how I lived my life, so naturally good things were happening to me.

my ego inflating by the second
and setting me up for a massive fall

We planned our life together. I introduced him to my children, who immediately liked him, my friends met him and of course my sister Louise who lived with me, she loved him straight away.

I once again overlooked some of the things he said or did that bothered me and completely ignored the fact that his now ex-girlfriend still lived with him. This meant he could visit me, but I couldn't visit him unless we went to a hotel, which we did in Amsterdam and Haarlem. Mainly though he came to me and although I knew it was odd, I was too in love with him to let anything ruin my euphoria.

nothing was rocking my boat

If I felt insecure, I told him and he'd reassure me it was all ok, he loved me and everything was coming together, but the anxiety I'd worked so hard to be free of was back with a vengeance and a million times worse. I put it down to the intensity of our love. I felt peaceful when he was with me and extremely anxious when he wasn't. Deep down I knew it wasn't healthy to feel this way.

eh you think?

It was borderline obsession, but he constantly told me he felt the same way.

I love you, you're everything to me

His words would soothe me temporarily, but the anxiety always returned. I'd learn to value actions over words, but that came later and I know what you're thinking, the writing was on the wall.

I knew that too, but I chose not to see it

We didn't spend Christmas together because his ex-girlfriend didn't want to be alone,

and I still chose not to see it

but he came for five glorious days over New Year. We walked in the woods, hung out with my kids, cooked, drank wine and just enjoyed being with each other. One night while slow dancing in my kitchen, he asked me to close my eyes and imagine we were at our wedding. My family were on one side, his on the other and we were dancing to our wedding song.

yes I want that, let's get married now

At that moment,

pissed on white wine

I never felt more in love in my life and would have carved out my heart and handed it to him if he'd asked. The fact that 20 minutes after feeling this, we had our first argument when he began heavily flirting with my sister's friend while I sat beside him.

It was fine, he didn't mean it

When I pointed out what he was doing, he didn't like being called on his behaviour and sloped off to bed. Of course I brushed it off and didn't mention it again.

At midnight on New Year's Eve wrapped tightly around each other, we watched fireworks in the distance from the hot tub in my garden and talked about the next day being the beginning of forever. We were going to build a house in Holland, my kids would come and go, and everything would be amazing. We even talked about having a baby together, a little girl and we'd call her Rose. It was one of the happiest moments of my life.

but a moment was all I got

The next day wasn't actually the beginning of forever; it was the beginning of the end.

and I didn't see it coming in a million years

He went back to Holland the next morning

not taking any of the Christmas presents I bought for him.

and within a few hours of saying goodbye to him at the airport, something changed. His dog had to be put down and he was distraught, but there was something else, I just couldn't put my finger on it. He seemed distant and cold, unavailable and suddenly not as interested as he'd been. There was no text to tell me he got home and I instinctively knew something was wrong.

My anxiety was through the roof, but I told myself it was just his grief at losing the dog, all was okay. I felt sad for him but couldn't comprehend what he was going through. Still somewhat emotionally closed down, I didn't understand the pain of loss and I didn't know grief so was unable to relate. I had a dog, I loved my dog and if he died I'd be sad, but not like this. He was devastated.

204

it's a dog, get over it

I tried to shake off my descent into absolute terror by going out with my sister. It was New Year's Day so we went down the pub and got absolutely smashed. As the day went on, my spidey senses were on high alert. I hadn't come this far on my journey to ignore my instinct completely, but I was overriding it by texting him as normal. This time however and for the first time since I met him, he ignored my texts completely and a cold dread swept through my body.

When he texted me the next day, he jokingly called me a stalker, because I'd sent him 17 text messages

in my drunken haze

and just reading those words burst the bubble. Suddenly I was self-conscious and embarrassed, something I'd never felt with him before. He said he was ok, devastated about his dog but he'd be in touch soon and it was like talking to a stranger. As I read the text, I felt myself plunging into panic mode.

For the next two weeks, I barely heard from him. I'd text here and there to ask if he was ok, but he'd ignore them or answer with one word responses. When I finally spoke to him on FaceTime two weeks later he promised everything was fine between us, but he was different. He was distant and distracted and seemed irritated at having to explain himself to me.

When we hung up from that call, I got into the shower and finally broke down. I cried like I'd never cried before. Tears poured down my face as water ran down my body and I stayed there until the water ran cold, absolutely sobbing. I was devastated that in his grief he hadn't turned to me, he'd shut me out and for the first time since I met him, I was unsure of his feelings towards me. He kept saying he loved me, but if that was true how could he treat me like this?

Completely confused, the only thing that kept me sane was my yoga. I'd go to my daily practice, return home, have a shower and breakdown sobbing. Somewhere in the midst of my tears, I thought at least I could finally cry.

silver lining

Maybe by releasing these tears, I'd soften the blow if the worst did happen because my instinct told me I was losing him. I just prayed it was wrong.

Until then, I thought I knew what emotional pain was. I soon learned that I didn't actually know the meaning of it. I didn't know my little breakdown in the shower was only the beginning of pain so unimaginable that it would almost destroy me.

206

24: The Profound Lesson

Maktub - It is Written
- ***Paul Coelho***

It was late in January when he came back to me but something about him had changed. I could tell he was avoiding something and the way he spoke to me felt different. It was as if our connection had dimmed.

I took it all in, but didn't say anything

I'd spent a few weeks thinking about it and had already decided to let him go. I'd done too much work on myself to go through this shit, my anxiety was still through the roof and my life was being consumed by him. I thought of nothing except him, loving him or losing him, our future together, our future apart, him loving me or not?

him living with his ex,
him never being available to talk to me,
him not returning my text messages

I was losing my mind and I couldn't do it anymore.

Having finally discovered my purpose in life, I'd been on track, excited and enthusiastic about my future, now it was completely overshadowed by my chaotic emotional state and although I was still speaking and writing,

a bit

my heart wasn't in it and my mind was all over the place. I was going crazy trying to understand what the fuck was going on and how the fuck romantic love had firmly reclaimed its position as the pinnacle of my life. Everything else was fading into the background and as I had in my marriage and any other relationships I'd even been in, I began disappearing into the man I loved.

This time however, I was self-aware enough to notice it.

ha! you're not getting off that easy!

I knew we were out of balance. I knew I was giving him everything, my heart and soul, my time, my love and understanding and I was getting a 10 minute chat whenever he had the time. I was frantic for something real from him, his words said 'love' but his actions said 'lies' and I was out of my mind.

liar, liar pants on fire

We'd gone from talking all the time on Facetime, to him being too busy at work and I could tell he was pulling back. In moments of sanity I knew loving someone wasn't supposed to feel like this

I didn't actually know what it was supposed to feel like

and before I met him I'd felt peace, something I hadn't thought possible for me. Now it had all gone to shit and I was once again crippled with anxiety and instead of love lifting me up,

only it wasn't love

it was tearing me down and I was dying.

I had half of what I always wanted, my heart was bursting with love for him, and that part felt right, but the situation felt wrong. He did love me, I was certain of that but he was uncertain about changing his life and that was the problem. No one in his life knew about me, except his ex-girlfriend and his mother.

I was his dirty little secret

He said he hadn't told his friends out of respect for his ex-girlfriend and I desperately wanted to believe that, but deep in my heart I knew it was bullshit. In reality he was unsure if he wanted to make the final leap and completely change his life. A life he told me he loved, the only thing missing in it was me.

When he arrived at my house three weeks after he started shutting me out, he was tired, so we had a couple of beers and went straight to bed. We made love all night and it felt deeply intimate so by the next morning, I'd managed to talk myself out of everything. Maybe I was wrong because surely you couldn't love someone so sweetly with your body, if you didn't love them deeply with your mind.

again my naivety was adorable

We enjoyed being together for the weekend and on Sunday just before he left to go home, we went for a walk in the woods. I told him I couldn't go on like this and needed to know if we were together or not. I explained that without drama, we could call it a day. I told him I could see his conflict, it was very apparent and that if my dog had died, the only person I would have turned to was him. Shutting me out had said so much and although I loved him, I couldn't live this way anymore, it was killing me.

It had been nine months since we met and we still weren't a proper couple. If we had been, he'd be spending more time in the UK and I'd be spending more time in Holland with him, in his home.

not in a hotel somewhere hiding from his friends and family

He looked at me and said something that didn't click with me until a few months later, 'It's no good', he said, 'I've fallen in love with you all over again.' At the time I was too preoccupied to notice, but afterward I thought about it,

a lot

'I've fallen in love with you all over again.' When had he fallen out of love with me?

in between New Years eve
and the end of January obviously

Standing in the woods he sobbed and told me he absolutely could not live his life without me in it. I asked if he was certain and he vowed he was. I was it, the love of his life, I was his everything and he couldn't let me go. With tears streaming down my face, I fell into his arms as relief flooded through my body and we both held each other crying in the middle of the woods,

like a couple of babies

with everyone passing by watching us. I didn't care, my happiness was restored and obviously I was a crazy irrational bitch who'd been overthinking the whole thing. He loved me, he picked me and everything was A okay.

210

When we got back to my house, I excitedly told my sons they'd be spending the summer in Holland. We'd be staying in Dutchboy's house and he'd show us around The Netherlands. They were fine with that. We already had family in Alkmaar and we could see them too. It was all good and I was excited.

I booked myself a flight for two weeks later. He was finally going to introduce me to his life, to his friends and show me where he lived. His ex-girlfriend was buying a house and moving on and our life together would really begin.

finally

I ignored the tiny bit of unease I felt. I wanted this and he wanted this. He looked me in the eye and said he couldn't live without me. We were spending our life together, he was my new dream and when I didn't have my children, I'd be in Holland and when I did, he'd be in the UK.

He'd chosen me so I told my gut instinct to fuck off.

a healthy and self realised approach

I refused to acknowledge or even bring up any of his recent behaviour. How he'd made me feel by ignoring me and shutting me out these past weeks, what that said about him as a man and what it had done to me. I kept telling myself it would all be ok in the end. I was playing the long game. He'd soon be mine and then we'd sort through everything.

When his flight was cancelled due to fog, he had an extra night so we went out and celebrated with my sister.

211

first he had to go outside
and call his ex-girlfriend,
but that was just a work thing

Having only one brother, he told Louise how happy he was to now have a sister and every word he said reinforced my happiness. Plans were made for him to meet the rest of my family in Dublin and the next day when I dropped him off at the airport, he kissed me and once again told me how much he loved me. However a few hours later something changed again and I felt like I had whiplash.

He Facetimed me four times that day and asked if it was definitely the right time for me to come to Holland. Reminding me of a caged tiger pacing back and forth, when he asked if we could delay meeting his friends and so on, I convinced him that it would all be ok. I told him the only thing that mattered was our love for each other and that we'd figure everything else out together.

throw, throw, throw yourself at him

I thought if I just got to Holland and the secret was out, he'd get over his fear of change and everything would be ok, but of course I was wrong. I should have walked away,

and regularly kicked myself for not doing so

I knew I was begging for a place in his life, but he fucking wanted it. I gave him the chance to walk away and he cried in the woods and told me he couldn't live without me, What the fuck was going on?

212

Two weeks later when I landed at Schiphol Airport, he was waiting for me wearing dark blue jeans, a navy jumper and smart leather boots. His hair was long on top and freshly washed. He looked gorgeous. When he kissed me, he smelt so good and I prayed to God, begged for my instinct to be wrong, because I was deeply in love with him and knew if this fell apart, my life was over.

We went to a hotel because his ex was still living in his house,

> *but she was looking for a new house,*
> *so this was the last time! promise*

When we checked in, we wandered around the city and then stopped at an Irish pub. He kept kissing me, looking at me with wonder in his eyes and telling me how beautiful I was and how much he loved me. It felt like the truth even though something in me screamed, SOMETHING IS WRONG. We made love all weekend but he was different. He was cold towards me and for the first time since I met him, he slept with his back to me instead of wrapping me in his arms. I never felt more insecure in my life, got horribly drunk and repeatedly asked him if he loved me.

> *do you love me? do you love me? do you love me?*

On the Saturday afternoon he left me in the pub alone and went to run an errand

> *ergo ring his girlfriend and discuss what I believe*
> *was their plan for him to dump me that weekend*

and I sat there for an hour, still denying anything was wrong. By the time he came back, I'd made friends with the people sitting next to me, trying to be popular and fun Suzanne who would

213

make a great girlfriend. He soon joined in and we had a great time.

Needless to say, I didn't meet any of his friends that weekend and I didn't get to see the town where he lived. He convinced me to wait a bit longer so we postponed it and although I knew what that meant, I absolutely refused to accept it. When he left me to sleep alone in the hotel on Sunday night, claiming he had an early start the next day, I began slipping into hell.

and still denied it

He dropped me to my cousin's pub in Alkmaar, but refused to come in and meet my family saying he was late and needed to get back and I told myself it was all okay, there'd be other times.

delusional

When I kissed him goodbye that night, I didn't know it would be the last time I'd ever see him. I didn't know I'd never kiss him again or feel the warmth of his arms wrapped around me. I sometimes wish I had. I might have taken more time to say goodbye. I might have memorised his face and captured the moment, but I was deep in denial and probably wouldn't have believed it anyway.

My body however knew and when I woke up the next morning, I was assaulted by anxiety on a scale I'd never experienced before. As I sat in the lobby of my hotel waiting for a taxi to take me to the airport, it took everything I had to remain calm. I'd come all the way to Holland and he couldn't even spend the last night with me or take me back to the airport. I knew something was very wrong.

At Schiphol airport I spent hours hyperventilating while trying to appear casual and lighthearted as I texted Dutchboy. I needed him to say something to make me feel better, to rid me of this feeling of impending doom, but of course his noticeable distance increased by the minute and I was at the edge of madness.

When I finally arrived home after a four hour delay, I was almost catatonic. I knew what was coming but I didn't want it. I really, really didn't want it.

25 The End - Again

Everything will be okay in the end and if it's not okay,
it's not the end.

    - **Anon**

For two weeks after that, he avoided me,

like the plague

claiming he was really busy with work and he couldn't talk. Still in denial, I tried to ask him about the holiday we'd talked about going on together.

majorly clutching at straws

We'd talked about going to the Florida Keys in the summer and I wanted to secure some dates with him. I thought by pinning him down and making plans, I'd override the feeling of inevitability. When he got impatient with me and said he didn't have time to even think about a holiday, I felt sick to my stomach and mortified by my actions.

I was so obvious

A few days later I told him I felt stupid for bringing it up and his response was that it was okay, just be patient and everything would be okay. He once again said he loved me and he just needed to get through this busy period.

Okay, phew for a minute there I thought
you were giving me the brush off

We talked on Facetime now and then but I could tell he wasn't into it. He kept saying he was really tired and stressed with work, but his texts were constant declarations of love. On Valentine's Day 12 beautiful red roses with a message that read, 'I love you,' signed Twin Flame, were delivered to my front door and once again relief coursed through me.

I was an idiot, of course he loved me

My instinct screamed it was over, but my head constantly overruled it. His actions said he was pulling back, but his words said he loved me. I was barely coherent with pain and confusion. I talked to Kate every day and every day she'd gently point out what was very obvious. I had to walk away. I already knew it and although I was ready to let him go a few weeks before, I couldn't do it anymore. He owned me, body and soul and I was lost.

Finally after a week of no contact at all,

as in, he completely ignored my (pretend everything is okay) good morning texts.

I told him that I knew something was wrong and we needed to talk. He agreed to Facetime on Tuesday morning after my yoga class and when he called, I could immediately tell something really was wrong. He was edgy and nervous. So with nothing left to lose, I was completely direct with him and asked what the fuck was going on. He said he felt unsure, he was stressed with work and couldn't think clearly, he had been talking to his ex-girlfriend and they found a way to reconnect.

reconnect?wtf?

'How the fuck can you reconnect with her, when you're deeply in love with me?' I asked, absolutely shocked at what he was saying. His look of guilt told me all I needed to know, so with a deep feeling of nausea and even though I didn't want to hear the answer, I asked. "Are you having sex with her again?" When he said it had happened once, the betrayal I felt nearly knocked me to the floor. Of all the things I'd expected to hear that morning, this was the last thing on my mind.

are you fucking kidding me?

He had categorically stated his relationship was over and told me he hadn't loved his ex for over a year before we met. He'd laughed out loud when I asked if they ever had intimacy the way we had, if they held hands and kissed like we did. "Never," he'd said, claiming their relationship was like brother and sister.

I couldn't work out if he lied to my face or if there was something wrong with him. Could his emotional intelligence really be this low? I listened as he tried to explain himself, then I asked what about us and all the plans we made? What about our life together, our wedding song in my kitchen, our dream house in Holland, our baby girl named Rose? I could have already been pregnant, because we never had anything other than unprotected sex, not caring if I got pregnant from day one. Even though my sons were teenagers, I wanted his baby, because we were forever and our daughter would be a part of that.

He didn't say anything. He just looked at me and when I asked him for an answer, he said again that he was stressed and confused and didn't know what he wanted.

eh! what the actual fuck?

218

I felt like I was in The Twilight Zone. He'd been telling me for months I was everything to him, that he loved me more than he'd ever loved anyone. Now he was telling me he'd been having sex with his ex. How could he do that?

quite easily apparently

Had it been happening the whole time we were together?

probably

I almost laughed out loud as I realised Karma is not bitch, it's a mirror. He'd cheated on his girlfriend with me nine months earlier and now he cheated on me with his girlfriend.

a real prince

The irony was excruciating. It took everything I had not to fall to my knees screaming in front of him. I asked him if I'd imagined the weekends of love we spent together. I reminded him of our conversation four weeks earlier, when he cried in the woods, told me I was the love of his fucking life and that he couldn't live without me.

His reply? We're nine months together and nothing has really changed.

what? wtf?

I looked at him in complete confusion as a million things ran through my mind. "What do you mean?" I whispered barely able to comprehend what was happening. He didn't answer me, just kept looking away and saying he was confused. I pointed out that I had been ready to go, I was in love with him, I was single,

219

living alone and excited at the thought of our life together. I wanted this relationship to work, even though we lived in different countries, I fucking loved him and didn't care that I had to book a flight and spend half a day travelling to see him.

Suddenly in the midst of all his bullshit, I finally accepted what I'd known for quite some time. He didn't want it anymore and he didn't want me. Somewhere along the line he'd changed his mind and I'd become a problem, something he had to deal with. I'd seen it in his behaviour towards me these past couple of months, but I'd denied it, unable to face the pain of my life without him. Now I could see it in his body language. He'd made his decision and there was nothing I could do about it.

He'd said so many times that he was excited by the idea of a life with me and that he felt alive for the first time in years, but when it came to the crunch, he couldn't do it, he couldn't commit and take a chance on something new.

the truth was excruciating

A sense of calm surrounded me and I figured I had nothing left to lose so told him exactly what was on my mind. I said ignoring my texts was just fucking rude, shutting me out of his life when he'd lost his dog was hurtful beyond words and that he was an absolute bastard for destroying what I believed was a sacred union between us. I actually believed we were something beyond love and would never in a million years have even looked at another man.

let alone fuck one

I was destroyed, but with amazing clarity could see how I'd tiptoed on eggshells for nine months, afraid of upsetting him, trying to fix him and gently coax him into changing his life. It had been the biggest waste of time and I couldn't work out if I was more pissed off at him for being a dick, or more pissed off at me for being so stupid.

Our favourite book was *The Alchemist* by Paul Cohello and we'd refer to it regularly, always looking for signs from the Universe together. 'Maktub' was our favourite phrase that meant 'it is written,' and we thought it referred to us. The story tells of a shepherd boy who follows signs from the Universe, sells his sheep and goes in search of his treasure. It's a hard path, but he knows that and while on it often wants to go back to his old life, give up on his quest and return to the safety of his sheep. We'd compare our lives to his. Talk about our path together being hard, but worth it in the end. Suddenly I realised it wasn't hard on my side, just his. I was always trying to make him see I was worth changing his life for, but in the end he went back to his sheep.

I considered fighting for him, I wanted to scream at him,

or punch him in the face

how could he do this to us? How could he treat me this way? Why did he not talk to me face to face while I was in Holland? Why did he not walk away when I gave him the chance? But I did none of that. I didn't stand up for myself and I didn't get the answers I needed.

which resulted in a lot of unnecessary pain
being unable to get closure

221

I swallowed it down like broken glass and said nothing. I just looked at him fidgeting in his empty office in Holland and I was consumed with sadness. He'd been my new dream, living my life with him was all I wanted and now our connection was severed, destroyed by cheating and lies. A part of me wanted to beg him to stay with me, but there was no point, I knew I could never get over the betrayal. I knew my only choice was to walk away.

We continued the conversation briefly, but I'd lost the ability to think straight and became painfully aware of blood pumping furiously around my body.

I thought I was going to faint

He didn't say he was sorry, didn't ask if I'd be ok, didn't say anything at all about me and focused only on how this was affecting his life. In the end,

and with a very wobbly voice

I told him I was going to make it very easy for him, that without any drama I'd walk away and he could go back to his life with his girlfriend. Then I looked at him for a few seconds, took in everything I loved about him, his handsome face, floppy hair and lovely green eyes. I even noticed how nice his navy shirt looked on him,

navy really was his colour

then I said goodbye, clicked the hang-up button and fell to the floor as my heart shattered into a billion pieces.

I screamed in pain, curled in a ball on the cold floor for what could have been an hour or five hours, while my dog Obi sat by my side licking the salty tears from my face. I couldn't move, I was dead, devoured by grief.

Eventually getting off the floor, I called Kate and relived the whole conversation with her. In between soul shattering sobs, I told her word for word what had happened and even though she knew it was coming,

we both did

she tried to calm me down with her amazing logic and reason. "You know this is the right thing honey, he didn't deserve to breathe the same air as you." I knew she was right but it didn't help. I couldn't comprehend the pain I was feeling, because I'd never felt anything like it before. Sorrow, betrayal, rejection, hurt, loss and abandonment all came close, but it was something deeper than that. I felt as if my soul had been ripped from my body and a part of me had died forever. How had this happened? I was self realized, damn it!

26: Emotional Death

Death is a stripping away of all that is not you.
The secret of life is to die before you die
and find that there is no death.
*-   **Eckhart Tolle***

The first week was the hardest. I'd close my eyes at night and see his face. If I was lucky enough to sleep, he was in my dreams. In the morning when I opened my eyes, for a split second I was free of him until reality hit and the pain annihilated me.

He was gone. There were no more texts of love, no more weekends walking around London, no more plans to be made. My dream of living in Holland was destroyed along with my sense of self-worth and nothing would ever be the same again. Most days I could barely breathe. I was suffocating and drenched in sorrow, unable to believe he'd left me. I'd been so sure he was my happy ending, my life partner and my forever. We were twin flames who'd found each other in an infinite Universe. So what the fuck had happened?

he lied and cheated on you

The dream of him was gone, ripped out of me along with my heart and with an intensity of indifference that only grief can cause, I didn't care about anything. Whatever I'd deemed important was completely irrelevant and no matter how hard I tried, I had no enthusiasm for my life.

Each morning I'd wake up and my mind would play and replay the last nine months. I'd wonder if I was going mad, was any of it real, did I imagine it? I wanted it so badly and was determined nothing would stand in my way. I knew I pushed hard, but I thought he loved me as much as I loved him. To realise it was all a lie was agony and if I could have laughed at my naivety I would have, but there was no laughter in me, only tears.

so many tears but at least I could now cry, winning

At 5am every morning, I'd walk my dog with music in my ears, *Iris* by the Goo Goo Dolls, on repeat, ten times, maybe twenty. 'And I'd give up forever to touch you, cause I know that you feel me somehow.'

I couldn't get that song out of my head

Then I'd listen to Eckhart Tolle, the spiritual teacher who'd given me so much comfort over the years, but this time his words of surrender meant nothing. I tried to be in the present moment, I tried to accept it was over and that it had happened for a reason, I tried to appreciate all that I still had, but I couldn't. It was too hard, my heart was broken and I missed him so badly.

He said I was everything, now I was nothing. Sometimes I'd be folding laundry and not notice I was sobbing, other times I'd fall to my knees screaming as pain ripped through me. I'd beg for help, someone to take the pain away.

but there was no one there,
I had to endure this alone,
it was part of my journey

Having read thousands of romantic books over the years, I'd never been able to understand 'book-love pain.' Now I knew exactly how it felt.

225

I couldn't tell anyone how I actually felt because I was incapable of verbalising it. Kate knew to some extent what I was going through but even then, having never experienced anything like it, she was unable to relate.

Something she told me a couple of years later
when a similar thing happened to her

I couldn't see beyond the love I felt for him, the love I wanted so badly and the love I lost. I'd often think about my favourite poem, Funeral Blues by W.H Auden and almost laugh at how relevant it had become to my life because it felt like he'd died.

I was broken. My worst fear had been realised and he was gone. He'd left me and I could barely say it out loud. Thankfully my self-awareness would help me through the haze of anguish. I was supposed to learn something very important from this, I just didn't know what it was.

yet

I recognised that once again, I'd forgotten about me. I'd disappeared into the man I loved and focused all my energy on his wants and needs. This time however, the Universe said no. It responded, 'Do you want to grow and become the best version of yourself Suzanne? Ok here it is, here's something that will be so hard to overcome, you'll grow beyond anything you ever imagined possible.'

I didn't want this lesson,
I just wanted to go back to
being happy and in love

Even though I was becoming a more authentic version of myself,

226

I simply would not learn this lesson and the pattern of behaviour would repeat itself until I did. It took desperate measures for me to realise this. I wanted to feel whole and healed, I wanted the peace that came with being true to who I was and I wanted to love myself completely. Falling in love with Dutchboy made me forget that. It made me crazy and the pain I was experiencing was my teacher.

I had two choices: I could learn from it and grow, or I could curl up and die. This pain would set me free, but first? First, the fires of hell.

PART 3 - REBIRTH

27: Grief

Sometimes it's OK if the only thing
you did today was breathe.
- ***Yumi Sakugawa***

When my marriage ended, my world was obliterated and I faced debilitating fear. The pain was deep enough to awaken me, force me onto a path of self-realisation and my journey began. The girl I was before died, a girl immersed in an illusion of life, filled with fear and self-loathing and one who needed validation for simply existing. She was gone forever and a new version of me was born.

As I grew into my second life, I learned about self-realisation, self-care and self-love. I was excited and enthusiastic about my discoveries and wanted to share it with the world. I was confident in my knowledge and felt a bit superior in my wisdom.

I mean, come on! I'd worked it out,
I knew the meaning of life

I desired praise and recognition and although I didn't realise it at the time, I wanted to help people more for my own success, than for their wellbeing. My dreams of being a great spiritual teacher were to fill a void in me, one I didn't know still existed. I thought I was self-realised, the work was done and I was free of the everyday afflictions of those still trapped by their ego.

Guru Suzanne

Fast forward a couple of years and I fell in love. My gift from the Universe, a prize for an enlightened soul such as mine and my happy ending. A gift it was, just not one I could ever have imagined. I could never have dreamed the Universe would do me such a favour, one that would transform my life completely, by helping me learn about the different types of pain.

The pain of fear. Something I'd experienced for most of my life that manifested through anxiety. It came to a head when my marriage ended and I crumbled beneath it. The fear of the unknown, the fear of being alone, the fear of being ordinary and never being enough. The fear of never making something of my life held me captive for years. Fear, fear, fear, I was consumed by it. However, through my journey of self-awareness, I learned to recognise the illusion of fear, make adjustments to my life and become less affected by it. When fear struck which it still did, I could rationalise it and overcome it more easily.

The other kind of pain and something that had hit me like a high speed freight train was the unimaginable pain of grief. My love was gone, as if he'd died, only it was worse, because he chose to walk away and leave me in hell. There were no words to describe how I felt. I was living on the edge of madness, unable to believe what had happened. He loved me so much and never wanted to be without me. Then he changed his mind.

somebody help me, please

Some nights I'd dream about him. I'd float out of my body and see the ocean beneath me as I'd drift up the coastline of Holland, into his town and then into his house. Seeing him asleep in bed, I'd slip in beside him, wrap myself in his arms and kiss him.

creepy I know, but I was hurting

I'd whisper his name until he opened his eyes and saw me, then with a startled look on his face, he'd disappear in a puff of smoke

230

and I'd wake up wrecked, desperate to text him and beg him to come back to me.

I wanted to tell him that I missed him, that I was sick with a broken heart and tormented by the fact that he didn't love me anymore. It was too much to take and like a zombie going through life, I could only do the bare minimum to get through the day. Getting the kids to school, I usually tidied the house, then went back to bed to cry for hours.

I couldn't eat, so I lost weight.

bonus

Most nights I couldn't sleep and lay in bed thinking about him, wondering if he was thinking about me. Why did he leave me? What had happened to make him change his mind? Had any of it been real, had he ever loved me? When the shock wore off, I wanted some answers so I texted him to see if we could talk. I asked for a few minutes of his time and of course he ignored my texts which utterly destroyed me. Never had I felt more desperate in my life. I was betrayed, abandoned, rejected and forgotten about.

all the good bits of a breakup

Sometimes while grocery shopping, I'd burst into tears if I saw something he liked to eat. If someone mentioned Holland, I'd cry. Sometimes I'd cry my way through yoga and every night I'd cry myself into a deeply disturbed, semi-conscious state of something that resembled sleep.

only to wake up a couple of hours later and cry again

A week after we broke up, I was in London with some girlfriends for lunch. Although I was struggling to socialise, I tried to pull myself together and after a very nice lunch to celebrate Kate's 40th birthday, we went to a wine bar for Porn Star Martinis. While sipping on my second or third one I had a complete breakdown. Heartfelt sorrow and tears of anguish poured down my face, instigated by nothing except my misery.

and the alcohol

My friends stared open mouthed, absolutely horrified. They'd never seen this side of me and quite simply didn't know what to do. I couldn't stop crying. I didn't have anything left in me to care about what they thought. I kept thinking about the plans we'd made, the life we were going to have together and how I'd lost the deepest love of my life.

As the weeks went on, it didn't get easier but I learned to live with it. I knew on some level that being broken was a good place to be, something I'd told many of my life coaching clients. When you hit rock bottom, the only way is up and I got that, but I wasn't on my way up yet, I needed to stay at rock bottom for a while. I had to sit with this pain and allow myself to go through the heartache. In the past I'd normally push pain away, now I was trying to live with it, breathe it in and process it.

progress

I couldn't work. Writing, life coaching and speaking became impossible and I cancelled any immediate appointments. How could I speak about being the best version of you when I was dying inside? Getting through the day became my only goal so I dedicated myself to my sons and focused solely on them. They were my anchor and even though they were devastated at seeing me in such pain, they were amazingly supportive. I deliberately didn't hide my feelings from them as I wanted them to witness emotional pain and know that life goes on. I did minimise the depth of it though, trying to be as normal as possible when they were home.

and falling to pieces when they weren't

Unusually helpful around the house, they'd offer to empty the dishwasher or walk the dog without me having to ask. Ethan even made cups of tea, bringing them to me in bed and his sweetness had me bawling like a baby.

If Kate hadn't been there, I would have sunk and never surfaced again. She rang me every day to talk through whatever I was feeling. We'd take it apart, analyse it, go through it with a fine-tooth comb, question motives, truths, statements and behaviour. Then put it all back together again. This helped me feel better, even if it was only for a couple of hours. In moments of acceptance, I knew everything happened for a reason, but they were fleeting moments. Mostly I felt shattered.

Socialising or even just speaking to people was incredibly difficult because my heart was so badly broken. I felt as if I'd been through a physical trauma, was critically injured and bleeding on the inside. Engaging in normal everyday life felt impossible.

A few weeks after he left and quite by accident, I got the chance to go to Mauritius. Kate had broken up with her partner and with a holiday already booked, I went in his place. We got to the island on a sunny Saturday morning in March, walked through the doors of our beautiful hotel and eight days later, walked through them again, into a taxi and back to the airport. We didn't

233

sightsee or do any tours of the island, we just stayed in the hotel, sunbathing, reading books, talking about life and love, going for long walks on the beach, eating delicious food, drinking far too much wine and crying. It was exactly what we needed and we didn't speak to anyone except a waiter to order a drink.

like the broken hearts club

I experienced all the stages of grief. Shock, denial, pain, guilt, anger, bargaining, depression, loneliness, reflection and finally acceptance. Initially I felt as if I was going through them all at the same time.

except acceptance

Shocked at what had happened, when that wore off, I was in the deepest pain. The denial came and went. I'd tell myself he'd be back any day now. He'd realise his mistake and turn up at my front door. Of course, I'd take him back, but only after he'd worked for it.

I bargained with God; please give him back to me, I'd do anything, sell my soul if I had to. Depression was always there, the underlying emotion that was present every day and of course, my self-loathing kicked in. I'd ask myself what was wrong with me? How could he treat me this way? Was I never to find love and keep it? Unable to reach acceptance, except for a moment here and there, it would eventually come, but I was too deeply entrenched in my pain to think about that.

Sometimes I'd check his WhatsApp status to see if he was online.

weirdo

Just knowing he was on his phone meant he was ok and that gave me peace. Other times, I felt so angry at him for how he treated me, his shocking lack of integrity and display of incredible cruelty by not returning my desperate texts messages was devastating. Throughout our relationship, I told him to always punch me with the truth and never kiss me with a lie. He'd kissed me with lies for nine months and I fell for every one of them.

hook, line and sinker

As time went on, the feeling of living with so much pain and trying to function normally was a strange experience. On the outside, I looked okay, but the sense of dread I carried and the physical ache in my heart was excruciating. To everyone else, it looked as if I was just getting on with it and although I was to some extent, there were triggers. I could never listen to our songs again and I could never look at the photos of us together, we looked so happy in them.

sob

Taking the advice of every book I'd ever read about emotional pain, I tried to take my mind off it. I gradually immersed myself in work and even though it was hard to focus, I felt better. I found myself writing articles about heartache and pain and was surprised by the quality of my writing. When quite unexpectedly my finances took a turn for the better, I decided to travel.

run

My kids were busy at boarding school, I had a lot of free time and I thought that if I moved around, maybe I'd be distracted from the intensity of pain, but of course I was wrong.

235

28: Running

Pain in this life is not avoidable,
but the pain we create avoiding pain is avoidable.
- ***R.D. Laing***

Consciously making the decision to travel, suddenly I was bombarded with invitations from all over the world. Friends inviting me for weekends away and family inviting me to visit. I smiled as I accepted, knowing full well the Universe was at work.

we were connected, what could I say!

I wanted to get as far away from Holland as possible, put distance between us, visit different countries and meet new people. I thought it might distract me and ease my heartache, but it didn't. It made it worse by magnifying the fact that I was meeting new people and enjoying different countries, without my love by my side and I was miserable.

fuck

After Mauritius, I went to Tenerife with my ex-husband and our sons. We rented a house over the Easter holiday and enjoyed glorious weather, good food, great wine and plenty of relaxation. I was reading *The Bhagavad Gita* and listening to it at the same time on Audible. I didn't want to miss one word that might help keep the panic, that was threatening to consume me, at bay. I was also reading *The Untethered Soul*, but couldn't bring myself to even consider the heart opening practice that helped me so much in the past. I was too deep in my pain to even want to be free of it.

The house we rented was owned by a Dutch lady and when she came to welcome us, I sobbed. My ex-husband was amazingly supportive and together with my sons, they treated me very gently for a week and I was grateful.

After that I went to Dublin a couple of times. I went to see my family first, then had a girlie weekend. Each time I tried

and failed

not to think about him. When I took the kids to Geneva and spent five days exploring the lake and enjoying the peace of Switzerland. I tried again

and failed

not to think of him.

In between my trips abroad, I decided I needed to date again. Maybe rebounding might rid me of this broken heart. It was almost six months and I still wasn't over him. Surely this kind of pain couldn't last too much longer.

how naive I was

Dating in general was a nightmare, but I met one nice guy, we connected and had a lovely day out in London. He was fun and attractive, but when he walked me to the tube and kissed me goodnight, I froze. A surge of panic threatened to knock me off my feet and even though I initially tried to kiss him back, I couldn't do it. I felt dead inside and kissing anyone other than my Dutchboy felt wrong. When I left, I cried all the way home, missing him more than ever.

After that my sister suggested a road trip to Canada, Colorado and New York. My kids were away with their father and I had three free weeks. Canada was wonderful. We flew to Toronto, did some sightseeing and then travelled to Ottawa to stay with family on my mother's side. Feeling very welcomed, they took such good care of us, entertained us, showed us beautiful Canada and supplied us with far too many supersonic gin & tonics.

you know who you are!

Colorado was amazing and having read about it in many romance novels over the years, my sister and I were uber excited to get there. Hoping to bag a couple of cowboys, we were single and ready to mingle.

I felt that on good days

My cousin Robert, on my dad's side invited us to stay,

being Irish means you have family everywhere

and showed us a fantastic time. He lived in Denver and we travelled to Boulder, Breckenridge and Vail. We didn't find any cowboys, but we had a lot of fun.

Arriving in New York for the last four days of our trip, I was tired, hungover and worn out. Although I was enjoying the trip of a lifetime with my sister, my anxiety was through the roof and I felt as if I was hanging on by a thread.

your average lighthearted holiday mood

Desperately trying to ignore it, I did some sightseeing with my sister, then of course we hit the bars and needless to say got

238

mindlessly drunk. When I woke up the next morning, the thread I was hanging onto snapped and I plummeted headfirst over the edge.

I woke early as always and was assaulted by such terror that I practically crawled out of bed. My sister was still fast asleep so rather than disturb her, I went to the rooftop pool in our hotel. It was 9am in NYC and already hotter than hell, so I sat on a lounger and desperately tried to breathe my way through the besiege of emotions. Over and over I reassured myself that I was safe, I was happy, and I was loved, while quietly observing the other people by the pool. Once again I yearned for the peace I perceived them to have, but this time I observed myself yearning and knew it was deceptive. They might not be peaceful at all.

more progress

I'd been practicing transcendental meditation for about two years at this stage which had helped me through a lot of my emotional trauma, but not this time. After 20 minutes of chanting, my panic began to increase and I realised I was having a full blown panic attack.

similar to what I experienced in Dubai
many years before, but a million times worse

My mind was foggy, I had a buzzing sound in my ears and felt as if I was about to obliterate into a billion pieces.

Stumbling back downstairs to our room, I woke my sister, told her how I felt and when she saw the state I was in, she knew it was serious. She hotfooted to the deli on the corner to get me a brown paper bag. I spent half an hour breathing into it, trying to calm down and when she admitted to her own anxiety, we laughed at the ridiculousness of it. Why did we feel this way? There was nothing wrong, we were safe but still, I couldn't shake the feeling of despair.

Decided to go for a walk, we set off though Hell's Kitchen and in the grip of terror, on a sunny Friday morning in August, I had another massive epiphany.

the second one of my life

Like a scene from a movie, people walked past me and I saw them differently. It was as if time slowed down and the busyness of New York faded into the background. I felt peaceful and calm and like an out of body experience, saw the world differently.

it was kinda white and hazy

I had a glimpse of something beyond the chaos and for a split second, the people looked different too. The cute dresses and sharp suits of the workers were gone. I had a glimpse of the essence of the person. It's really hard to describe and I'm still not sure what happened, but something immediately shifted and the epiphany was this:

> Every person on this planet is the same as me. We are all in this together. We all go through the same shit, the same emotions, the same fears and the same worries. It doesn't matter if we're rich and famous, poor and unknown or what colour, race, sexuality or religion we are. We all die in the end and are for now just trying to get through life and find a bit of happiness.

I'd spent my whole life envying other people for having their shit together or having a better life than me. I thought I was alone in my chaos but suddenly I knew that simply wasn't true. The

240

people of New York were just like me, going through life every day, dealing with the same shit and striving for something better. All just doing whatever it takes to live a good life.

I felt at complete peace and wanted to stay in this realm of calmness, but less than a minute later I slammed back in my body. The liveliness of 57th on 8th Avenue became apparent again and I was kicked in the stomach by my anxiety...but something had changed.

what the fuck was that?

As I looked around, suddenly being in New York became irrelevant and I wanted to go home. I was tired of running around the world. I wanted to see my kids, be in my own bed, do yoga, write and think about what had just happened to me. I told my sister how I felt and she was more than happy to go, so six hours later we made our way to JFK, onto a cheap Norwegian Air flight and flew back to the UK, three days earlier than intended. It was freezing cold, lashing rain and I never felt as happy to be home in my life. My anxiety relaxed and as I reflected and wrote about what happened in New York, I felt a little better about my life.

it might not be that bad after all

I stayed at home for a few months until early October when I went to Norway for an Eckhart Tolle conference. As a huge fan of his teachings, I was very excited to be spending time in his company. His book, *The Power of Now*, had been a huge part of my awakening and had helped me so much in my life, so being in the same room as its author was a sublime experience.

I was completely starstruck

241

At a beautiful resort in the Norwegian countryside, I found a little more peace. Being hearing impaired meant I had a front row seat for the whole event and was ten feet from Eckhart. I felt deeply moved by the humility and peaceful presence of this man and desperately wanted to feel the same way.

I didn't know I was nearly there!

My heart was still severely broken, but I was learning to accept the present moment more and resist it less. Listening to every word Eckhart said that weekend, I knew with absolute certainty I was exactly where I was supposed to be in my life, even though I was alone and even though the extra ticket I'd bought for my ex-boyfriend to join me felt heavy in my bag, a birthday present he didn't get to use.

I was reminded that everything exists in the now, to look for answers within and bring challenges and problems back to the present moment. As I listened to him speak, I wondered what it must feel like to live in a place of complete peace. In the place I witnessed for a split second wandering around New York, free of torment, free from pain, with no need to seek answers, approval or validation and just align with the Universe.

sigh

Denmark was next on my hit list. I took my sons to visit our friends and we toured the beautiful city of Copenhagen, then we finished off the year with a family trip to Mexico. My ex-husband joined us and we spent two weeks in Cancun having a fantastic time. I still thought about my ex-boyfriend daily, but I was getting on with my life and I had moments of happiness.

242

even though I posted my travels on Facebook,
hoping he'd check and see the amazing life
I was pretending to have without him

29: Brutal Truth

The truth is rarely pure and never simple.
- ***Oscar Wilde***

Shortly before my trip to Norway, I began seeing a physiotherapist. As had happened many years before, I woke up one morning and the left side of my body was frozen. I knew it was activated by emotional trauma and was surprised it had taken so long to hit me.

I'd been in the midst of emotional trauma
for about eight months!

Once again it started in my neck and travelled down my arm and leg, it was incredibly painful and I was miserable. However my yoga was strong, so it didn't develop into full blown sciatica like last time and I was thankful for that.

My yoga teacher Terri recommended a physiotherapist who turned out to be a deeply spiritual woman

no surprise there

and our sessions turned into therapy. While she massaged my body, she helped open my mind even further and over the course of a few months, I was astonished at what I discovered about myself.

I was a seeker of truth.

no shit!

Until then I hadn't realised I needed truth in all aspects of my life

I just thought I was a crazy over thinker

and was knocked on my ass when she pointed it out to me. If I wasn't living my truth or speaking it, my anxiety was activated. Ironic that I'd always been unwilling to accept the truth of my life and had created an acceptable version of it that allowed me to stay in my comfort zone.

much easier that way

I was a master at bending the truth but lately it wouldn't bend so easily.

Before my awakening I could rationalise other people's behaviour towards me to avoid conflict and make myself feel better, but now I couldn't do it. The tricks I'd used weren't working anymore. Usually if someone took advantage of me, I'd make an excuse for their behaviour, telling myself I was okay with it, even though I wasn't.

It's fine, I'm sure they don't mean to

If a guy didn't return a text, I'd make an excuse that they were busy except no one is ever too busy to return a fucking text.

rude

If I didn't keep my word or let someone down, I'd tell myself they were fine with it, even though I knew they probably weren't. I didn't like facing up to things in my life, I didn't like having to explain myself to people, so would play down my importance to them.

they don't care if I cancel...again

I didn't like my inadequacies and my imperfections or the fact that I was a bit of a doormat, weak and unable to stand up for myself or say no. I glossed over all of that for years and told myself I was fine so many times, I almost believed it.

repeat after me. I'm fine, I'm fine, I'm fine

I had been trying to find my spiritual awakening on my terms. I'd been treading lightly, not going deep enough to really shake things up and never accepting the absolute truth of my life. Now I had no choice, because my version of how my life should go was destroyed. It was in tatters, my love was gone, my self-worth annihilated and my confidence destroyed. I had nothing left to lose. The stories I told myself to cope, suddenly became irrelevant and I had to stare the truth in the face.

Truth number one: the man I loved with all my heart had lied and cheated on me. He knew how desperately in love with him I was and he went along with it, too afraid to tell me he had doubts. He'd been backing away for months and although I suspected it, I refused to acknowledge it. When his dog died, he ignored me for two weeks and deep inside I believe he was sleeping with his ex-girlfriend again, while telling me I was the love of his life.

told you the truth would hurt

Truth number two: I never had him; I never actually had him.

246

sob

I wanted him so badly, but he was never mine. What began with dishonesty, ended with dishonesty and I chased after a fiction. A dream I created about us living in the land of happily ever after. When the voice of reason tried to intervene with whispers of, 'Are you sure you love him?' I told it to fuck off.

> *of course I loved him,*
> *we were the happiest couple to ever live*

One evening almost a year after our breakup I was miserable, lonely and drunk so I texted him to ask why he'd abandoned me and why he'd treated me so badly.

> *always a good idea when you're pissed on white wine*

I didn't often text because he didn't respond and that hurt too much. I also thought that by remaining aloof and distant, he'd miss me and come back. Now none of that mattered. I just wanted answers. This time he did respond and said, 'don't think any of this has been easy on me.' Once again it was about him. No apology, no asking if I was okay. I was devastated. I cried myself to sleep and was kicking myself the next morning for texting him.

Truth number three:

> *and this one was grueling*

throughout our whole relationship, I accepted him sharing a bed with his ex-girlfriend. He told me it was two single beds pushed together and there were no other

247

beds in his house, so in my desperation to keep him, I lied to myself about being okay with it.

don't be selfish Suzanne,
he can't sleep in the spare room!!

I should have walked away but I wasn't strong enough and didn't value myself enough to say no. I just accepted his behaviour, telling myself it would all change soon and we'd be together.

anything other than facing the truth
of what was actually going on

I was unaware of the pattern. If I wanted something I couldn't have, I'd be determined to get it. Something deep inside me said, 'challenge accepted,' and I'd need to prove to myself that I could either get what I wanted or I was unworthy of it. Persecuting myself over and over, I simply would not learn this lesson.

As a child, my mother would say I could never take no for an answer and I exhausted her with my demands. When I was 16 and chasing after my first boyfriend, I wouldn't accept that he didn't want me and threw myself at him, allowing him to use me for sex. The few short relationships I had since my marriage ended always saw me in pursuit. I either got them or had no choice but to scrape my dignity off the floor and admit defeat.

cringe

So there it was staring me in the face, truth number four: and it was that my need to be loved and wanted by someone was more important to me than my self-respect.

I'll say that again because it was especially soul destroying. My need to be loved and wanted by someone was more important to me than my self-respect.

and that ladies and gentlemen,
is what rock bottom looks like

I went after men who were unavailable because I needed to get them. When I got them, I usually discovered very quickly that I didn't want them after all. The reason? I was emotionally unavailable and unable to love in a functional way because I was unable to love myself. I'd been wearing a mask my whole life and when in a relationship, I became who I believed my lover needed me to be.

a compliant, submissive walkover

It was all bravado, fake confidence and false positivity. From the outside it looked as if I was in the driving seat of my relationships, but I wasn't. I gave the impression of having it together, but I was actually very insecure when it came to love.

The emotional deprivation I thought I'd dealt with during my time studying Kabbalah was still rife and forced me to prove myself undeserving of love. My self-awareness had improved, but my self-loathing was so deeply ingrained, that it took the trauma of losing what I believed to be the love of my life for me to recognise this.

a lesson or a blessing? definitely a lesson

I longed to be in love, but I was also terrified of it because what then? How could I create drama and prove myself unlovable, if I was actually in a loving relationship? My ex-husband had been the only man I hadn't pursued and I was incapable of loving him. When he told me he loved me, I didn't believe him because my dysfunctional perception of love prevented me from doing so. It convinced me that love had to be hard and I had to fight for it or it wasn't real. If it was too easy, it wouldn't last.

During our relationship, I told my Dutchman I'd be fine if he ever went back to his ex-girlfriend. I told him I was strong and would get over it.

I'd be A..OK mister

A defence mechanism that backfired, because on one level I thought he'd never leave me, but deep down,

very deep down

I knew he would. He wouldn't choose me, because he didn't love me enough and that hurt so much, but at least I was right.

da daaaaa

My worthlessness confirmed.

The ultimate truth was that I was lovable, worthy of love and I mattered. My beliefs were flawed and I was attracting situations to my life to confirm how I subconsciously felt about myself. I didn't want to do that anymore.

finally

250

Facing the truth was freeing me and with one truth, comes ten. The floodgates opened and suddenly I was besieged by them.

30: Self Realisation

Your own self realisation is the greatest service you can render the world.
-   ***Ramana Maharshi***

In the six months since I began accepting the absolute truth of my life, things really started to change. There was no more sugar coating, I knew what I knew and I couldn't un-know it. I could no longer pull the wool over my eyes or pretend to be okay if I wasn't.

a completely new experience for me

My need to fit in began to diminish and I was no longer agreeing with people just for the sake of it.

eek

The program was breaking and for the first time in my life I became aware of how easily I'd been persuaded to do what I didn't want to do, so I stopped. I began making choices based on what I wanted to do without too much explanation, rather than what I thought I should do.

To some, it looked a bit like arrogance, but it wasn't. It was confidence in the decisions I made about my life and even though my family and friends were a bit unsure about this new side of me, they understood it was part of my journey. I was less available, I wanted to be alone more, because interacting with people felt hard. I had a distinct lack of desire to explain what I was going through and I didn't want to talk about the realisations I was having on a daily basis.

252

very different from Suzanne the over-explainer

On top of that, I no longer needed approval or validation from anyone. In fact I needed nothing, I just wanted to process these new truths on my own without explanation or justification.

Pandora's box had sprung open and I was besieged by truths. The hardest one to take was that my broken heart had been the result of my obsessive determination to get what I wanted and my 'soul-mate' relationship had actually been a frenzied and unhealthy love affair.

ouch, ouch, ouch

Blinded by my obsession, I simply would not allow any outcome other than happy ever after and was so determined to get him, that I forgot why I wanted him in the first place. Had I even loved him? Yes, more than I had loved anyone in my life, but I still hadn't loved myself first and that had always been my biggest source of my suffering.

the people pleaser was finally being laid to rest

Truth number six or was it seven? I was an underachiever. I had a curious and enquiring mind, I was a fast learner and should have had professional success by now, but I held myself back due to my limiting beliefs. I was programmed to doubt myself and constantly ridiculed my own dreams of achievement.

achievement like that just doesn't happen to the likes of me

Truth number whatever: I was addicted to drama. My life without problems was incomprehensible, because what the fuck would I do if I wasn't focused on the problem? My spiritual work had helped me and over the years my outlook on life became generally more positive, but like an eagle seeking its prey, I searched for obstacles, stopping myself from achieving the life I wanted and until I recognised this, I could never change it.

Stumbling across a Ted Talk by Brene Brown about shame, I listened as she basically described my life.

shame? wtf?

As I listened, I realised I'd been ashamed for most of my life. Raised in a working class part of Dublin, as soon as I turned 18, I socialised in more upmarket neighbourhoods, embarrassed and ashamed of my social status. I

wrongly

believed people with money were better than me and relied on materialism for my sense of security. Money equaled safety and poverty had been a huge source of shame for me. I'd seen my mother worry about paying bills and witnessed her shame. The idea of having no money sent me spiraling into terror.

I was ashamed of what I perceived to be my failure and focused only on what I had yet to achieve, paying no attention to how far I'd come.

I was ashamed of my inadequacies and imperfections. No one got to see the real me. My Dutch boyfriend got closer than anyone, but even then I was trying to get him and showed only my best side. My husband of 12 years had never seen the real me, he'd seen a superficial side of me because at the time, I didn't know it was superficial.

unconscious incompetence:
you don't know what you don't know

I held a firm belief that I had to be strong, I had to be successful and I had to have my shit together to add value to the relationships in my life. I was ashamed of my weakness, my ordinariness. Who the fuck wanted ordinary? I strived to be extraordinary in everything I did. I needed to impress, excite, awe and thrill the people I met. Only then did I feel worthy of their time.

Having always pushed past my pain, when my marriage broke down I thought I'd die, but I didn't allow myself time to process it. Instead I berated myself, insisting I pull myself together, all the while being terrified of being smothered by it.

brush it off and bounce back

This time however, I hadn't bounced back. I honestly thought I'd be over this heartache in three months and 18 months later, I still thought about him and missed him every day. I was ashamed of myself for being so fucking pathetic.

With shame comes vulnerability, with vulnerability comes empathy and bingo, I had neither. I'd die rather than be vulnerable in front of anyone and that meant I had no empathy for myself or for others. It took my heart being smashed to smithereens for me to realise this. In the past I kept other people's pain at a distance, I was uncomfortable with it and unable to truly relate. Now that I'd experienced grief firsthand, my empathy was activated and I understood how utterly destroyed a person could be, because I felt it every day.

Very slowly I was realising I didn't have to be ashamed of anything. I didn't have to be ashamed of my weakness, my pain or my grief. There was no shame in having a broken heart. I was allowed to grieve for as long as I needed to. I was allowed to sit with my pain for as long as it took and I was allowed to break down and cry if I was hurting. I didn't have to hold it together. I was allowed to be imperfect and it was actually okay not to be okay.

finally I was having empathy for myself

In the months that followed, I became very comfortable with my vulnerability and would happily point out my weakness to the people I met. I felt no need to have it all figured out and began allowing my life to flow. That in itself was a miracle. I could just be me and the pain, chaos and imperfection were a part of who I was.

During one of my physiotherapy sessions while talking about my newfound empathy, my therapist asked if we could discuss my family.

sure, why not

She had previously said she thought it my responsibility to heal them, to bring us closer and function better and I laughed in her face.

that was seriously funny

I talked regularly about them, about my issues growing up, how I didn't feel close to them and felt unsupported in times of great pain.

256

verbally bashing and blaming them for all my shit

However, since living my truth and understanding the role of shame in my life, I now felt different about them. I realised they were just living their lives and it wasn't that they hadn't supported me and loved me through all my shit, I'd just been unable to receive it.

the martyr

I no longer felt the need to wear my family's dysfunction as a badge and had accepted we were on different pages. I needed spiritual realisation and they didn't. Over the years their lack of interest in my spiritual teachings had pissed me off. I'd recommend books and spiritual practices to change their lives that they'd simply ignore.

rude!

I'd tell my sisters they should do this, or my mother should do that to live a better life, but they lacked enthusiasm and I'd now come to terms with that. All was as it should be and after all, spirituality can't be forced. When the student is ready the teacher appears.

When I explained this to her, she casually said, "it sounds as though you weren't trying to help them, you were trying to control them because you're a control freak."

eh, what?

I beg your pardon, me a control freak? Ha, that truly was a joke, so I politely asked, "Ahem, what do you mean, a control freak?" I absolutely was not a control freak. My ex-husband was a control freak and I still wore that like a badge. I was easy going, a fly by the seat of my pants kinda gal who definitely wasn't a fucking control freak.

My life was disorganised chaos. I barely got the kids out to school on time, usually forgetting at least one gym bag on Monday morning. My utility room resembled something close to a Chinese laundry, where I could spend ten minutes looking for a pair of knickers. I sometimes missed parent meetings, forgot about early pickups, ran out of milk, regularly missed doctor and dentist appointments and the poor dog often missed a walk because I just couldn't fit it in. There were times when I wished I was a control freak. I might be more organised and in a self-righteous manner, I bloody well told her so.

"Not that kind of control freak," she said almost laughing, "You're an emotional control freak, who's always trying to control the uncontrollable."

again...what?

I sat gaping at her, feeling like she'd punched me in the stomach, because although I didn't exactly know what she meant by an emotional control freak, I absolutely knew that I was one.

Something deep within me recognised this and when I asked her to explain she said this, "Emotional control freaks focus on controlling the outcome of things they can't control and as a result cause their own pain. They usually suffer with excruciating anxiety, mild depression and stress."

sound familiar?

258

Like a wave crashing over me, I knew I was an emotional control freak. I'd spent my whole life trying to control the uncontrollable and I immediately knew the years of tearing myself apart with anxiety and fear were the result of my need for control. I needed to control everything that happened to me, everything I was feeling and everything that other people thought of me.

I thought about the many spiritual teachers I'd listened to over the years, in particular Eckhart Tolle's and his words of surrender. 'Let it go.' I knew this, I'd read about surrender in a million books. I talked about it all the time, told others to let go and practiced it to some degree in my own life,

I'd stopped caring what people thought of me

but I didn't know I was trying to control my emotions. I thought this was all happening *to* me. I was a victim of other people's behaviour when of course I was actually the victim of my own.

excruciating, I couldn't bear it

When I left my appointment that day, I was gobsmacked but something clicked into place and my life would quite simply never be the same. Overcome with a sense of calmness, I now realised what I tried to control and spent the next few weeks writing about it and processing it in my mind.

My family and the choices they made: I'd been judging them for not getting enough from their lives.

this is how I think you should live your life

I now realised they could live their lives however they wanted and it was none of my business.

What people thought of me: whatever was left of the people pleaser suddenly fell away as I realised people either liked me or they didn't. Either was okay with me.

My children and the choices they made: as they got older, I could guide and nurture them, but I couldn't control the choices they made, I could only cross my fingers and hope for the best.

My career: I could only do what I could do, I couldn't force it to happen. I could only work hard, do my best and release it to the Universe.

And of course that big one, love: someone either loved me or they didn't and I could not control a person's feelings for me, something I'd learned the hard way.

I realised I'd been forcing my life for as long as I could remember and not only was I an emotional control freak, I was a manipulative, emotional control freak. Always trying to sway things in my favour, I'd use charm, determination and coercion,

if I had to

to get what I wanted. It had become second nature to me and I had no idea I was doing it. I thought myself easygoing, gave the impression of being laid back and relaxed, but inside I burned with anxiety, trying to manipulate situations and trying to control my life and the lives of the people closest to me.

I pushed so hard to get my Dutchman to commit to me, that I inadvertently pushed him away. I tried to control everything. What we were going to do with our lives, when we'd see each other, how we'd live between Holland and the UK. What our friends would think, how his family would react. I planned and plotted until everything felt right in my head and if I didn't get his full compliance, my anxiety spiked and I sent myself into a frenzy.

The ridiculousness of it almost made me laugh, but the transparency I gained was breathtaking. Emotional control is an illusion. Shit happens, life changes, feelings change, people change, there's nothing I could do about any of that.

holy shit!!!

My perception had always been that certain things needed to happen in order for me to feel happy and safe. First, I had to fall in love.

no compromise

I needed to be successful and financially secure.

no compromise

My body had to be perfect.

no compromise

And I had to have the love and approval of everyone I met.

no compromise

For years, I'd literally made myself sick worrying if people liked me, if I'd said the right thing, if I'd looked fat or sounded stupid and the whole time, it had been out of my control. I'd judged people for not living as I thought they should, self-righteous in my opinions,

behind their back

and bossy in my need for them to fit into my perception of how they should live.

astonishing!

As with everything I learn about myself, I wanted to know more and began investigating emotional control and came across something called emotional perfectionism.

no, surely not

Yes, I was that as well. An emotional control freak and an emotional perfectionist.

perfect

An emotional perfectionist applies impossible standards to how they think they should feel, making daily statements like, I should be happy, I should be stronger, I shouldn't be upset. I can't let anyone see my sadness. They need to believe I'm coping.

these had been my usual daily affirmations

I'd unknowingly put ridiculous standards on myself every day and berated myself for years when I couldn't live up to them.

This was the biggest turning point in my journey. I had years and years of trying to control everything to work through. It wouldn't happen overnight but the process had begun and who I truly was, was beginning to emerge.

31: Letting Go

In the process of letting go,
you will lose many things from the past,
but you will find yourself.
     -   ***Deepak Chopra***

I had truth, I embraced my vulnerability, learned to be empathic towards myself and others and found out I was an emotional control freak. The first three happened naturally. I simply had no choice but to see the truth in every situation in my life.

the filter was gone

I was tired of projecting myself as the strongest person on the planet. If I needed a shoulder to cry on, I was ready to ask for it and I genuinely felt empathy for people in pain, so much so that I'd eventually have to learn to protect myself from taking on other people's pain, something that could affect me for days.

However, emotional control was the big one for me. Responsible for so much suffering in my life, it was deeply rooted into who I was and changing it would be the hardest thing I'd ever do. I knew what life looked like when you let go of control. I'd caught micro glimpses of it during my meditation and often thought about my experience in New York when I'd seen a flash of it, during my panic attack.

the panic attack of all panic attacks

I knew how to surrender when faced with challenges in my life. It might take a few hours of overthinking and anxiety, but I could change the state of my mind and let go, but here's the thing, the effect was temporary and the anxiety was never far away.

264

By recognising my need for emotional control, I now understood that what I thought was letting go, was only letting go of external stuff. I didn't go deep enough to make real change happen.

that scared the shit out of me

To fully let go I had to completely accept and love who I was, I had to accept my life as it was, embrace it and go with it. No more planning or plotting to distract myself, no giving in to the fear, no people pleasing, no putting responsibility for my happiness on anything or anyone and no more seeking romantic love to validate my very existence. Just full acceptance of how my life had turned out so far.

I knew what full acceptance was on an intellectual level. I'd read all the books, but I hadn't connected with it on an emotional level. I hadn't known my need for control was so deep seated that letting it go would be the most terrifying thing I'd ever do. The thought of not having a plan in place for how I thought my life should go was just ridiculous.

To give up control I had to jump off a cliff and free-fall. I had to accept my life going off plan and instead of frantically trying to manoeuvre it back on track and causing extreme anxiety, I had to let it go. This was what my journey had led to, this was what I wanted, instigated by the most painful thing I'd ever experienced. The Universe threw down the gauntlet. 'Okay Suzanne, you want this, you want to know who you are, to align with me and know absolute peace? Here it is, your move.'

It came in the form of heart shattering grief that stripped me bare, because only by going there could I access the deepest part of myself. What started out as the answer to every prayer I ever had, the love of my life, a love beyond imagination, ended up destroying me.

temporarily and for the most beautiful reason of all

I'd been bathing in my success, celebrating that fact that I got what everyone else wanted, true love. All those years of not settling had paid off and I felt so justified in the upheaval of my life. I was right, I fucking knew there was more for me. Then, in the midst of my megalomania it was ripped from me, torn away so violently, on FaceTime and with him in a different country with no hope of bumping into him to demand an explanation.

I fell hard,

off my high horse

devastated and broken. This time the Universe said enough and finally clobbered me with the lesson that would break the pattern.

control the illusion, create anxiety, repeat

I wanted the truth, I wanted to know myself without doubt or compromise, to love myself unconditionally and none of that was possible until I learned to let go. Okay I could do this. Surely letting go was not that hard?

it was the hardest thing I ever did, but I learned

I began observing myself, noticing when I was trying to control situations beyond my control and gently let go. Little things like worrying if I said the wrong thing to someone, instead of trying to explain what I meant, I just let it go. If I forgot to call someone back, I'd just text and say call you another time, instead of giving a hundred reasons why I forgot and just let it go.

It took practice, but it got easier with time and before long the blocks, barriers and hurdles I'd subconsciously placed in my path began to fade as I realised I didn't have to control anything. I wasn't emotionally responsible for anyone except myself and the pressure I put myself under for years melted away.

At first, I'd wake up each morning waiting for the sense of dread or the usual anxiety to kick in, thinking any minute now, but when it didn't happen, I was at first shocked, then surprised, then delighted.

where's the anxiety?

When days turned into weeks and it still didn't show up, I felt like I was walking in the clouds because years and years of anxiety was heavy. Now that it was gone, I felt like I was floating.

Very soon I realised what a busy body I was,

blush

always in other people's business, telling them how they should live. I felt embarrassed to discover my impatience played a significant role in my need for control. If I wanted something, I wanted it now. If I was asked for advice and gave it, I wanted to see it implemented immediately and got frustrated when it wasn't.

naturally bossy I was known to my friends

267

as Marge in charge

My three teenage sons were great practice for letting go. Accepting fully that I couldn't control the normal teenage drama, I let it go.

it was hard

They were going to experience it anyway and rather than trying to protect them or punish them for all the shit they got up to, I tried to understand what they were going through more. I tried to offer guidance and not to lose it when I had to shout up the stairs that dinner was ready, 22 fucking times. Instead I tried to talk to them in a calm manner, which they were completely suspicious of at first, being used to my usual reaction of shouting and screaming.

like a banshee on speed

I explained I no longer wanted to control their teenage drama and instead wanted to give better and more objective advice. They were still suspicious but soon shook their shoulders.

whatever, crazy woman

Quickly realising that letting go of emotional control allowed control in other areas of life, I began introducing soft rules and boundaries. If the boys were taking the piss, instead of an argument, I simply pointed out what they were doing, explained why it was unacceptable and bingo, it started to work. They started confiding in me more and asking my advice which was a bloody miracle. I was treating them differently and they liked it.

Letting go and saying no to others took time. I realised how much I took on, afraid to disappoint or upset people, then got pissed off at myself for doing so. Saying no without giving a million explanations was uncharted territory, but I soon got used to it.

If I wasn't invited somewhere, instead of feeling rejected or insecure, I let it go.
If I let someone down, once again I was sorry to disappoint, but I let it go.
If I went on a date and he didn't call me, I no longer questioned my worth, my looks, my body or my intelligence, I just let it go.
If I had a lazy day, instead of beating myself up, I let it go.
Someone reacting negatively towards me, I'd respond in a non-aggressive way, then let it go.

no more replaying conversations
in my head felt so liberating

My family! When I finally let go of trying to control how I thought they should live, my relationship with them transformed. My therapist was somewhat correct. It wasn't my responsibility to heal them, it was my responsibility to heal me. When that happened, everything clicked into place.

At first I seemed a bit detached, I wasn't calling as much and I didn't question anything. If someone cancelled or let me down, I didn't care. The more I practiced letting go of thoughts that caused my suffering, the less internal chatter I had. Instead of sensationalising situations or thinking the worst, I saw them for what they were and let go of everything else. I was no longer sweating the small stuff and soon that became easy and I began letting go of the big stuff.

My Dutch boyfriend leaving me didn't matter anymore. I'd hung on for almost two years, destroyed by his behaviour towards me and now I couldn't work out what hurt the most. Him leaving me, or me failing to get him and therefore looking stupid to all my friends.

probably the latter

Whichever it was, it washed away and I no longer cared about it, I just let it go.

Two years and two months after he left me, I met him for a drink in Holland. I hadn't seen a trace of him in all that time and when I walked into the bar and saw him sitting in the garden, I smiled. He was lovely and there was a familiarity about him, but I didn't feel love. That girl he knew had been to hell and back and she didn't exist anymore. We hugged and he told me he was sorry for everything he put me through.

finally, I got the words

He said he just couldn't change his life and was terrified that if he did, I'd give up on him and as I listened to him, I realised he was probably right.

I told him I forgave him and that falling in love with him had enabled me to fall in love with me. He'd given me the gift of empathy and compassion, self-love and forgiveness. He'd forced me to endure the deepest pain of my life, but I was so grateful, because in the end, it changed the blueprint of who I was.

Loving and losing him helped me realise my need for control, because on days when I screamed in pain, broken and desperate to hear from him, there was nothing I could do about it, I had to let it go. He truly was a gift from the Universe, just not in the way I had initially thought. Without him, I would have continued in my cycle of emotional dysfunction, chasing after the unattainable, proving myself unworthy and never pushing far enough to discover who I was.

When I left him that day, I felt happier than ever before as any trace of 'what if' evaporated. I knew he was never the man for me and had come into my life to teach me the hardest lesson of all. One I'd finally learned and I was free of him at last.

hallelujah

After that everything else began to fall away. My dysfunctional childhood, something I'd carried for most of my life drained away and I wondered what the fuss had been about. What I perceived as emotional deprivation had defined my life. I was so caught up in what I thought my childhood should have looked like, in order for me to be happy, that I missed the point. I was loved as a child, my mother and father loved me so much and still do, I just couldn't accept it. I blocked their love and used what I perceived as my dysfunctional childhood to justify the pain of not being worthy of real love, but none of it mattered anymore.

Fear; the single biggest block of my life had kept me paralysed for years. I allowed my fear of failure, of looking stupid, of being alone, fat, poor or miserable to determine my life. Trying to control the outcome of everything, I'd sidestepped risk,

by playing safe in my opinions

fended off judgement,

by trying hard to be liked by everyone

bypassed loneliness,

by trying to force love

I hung onto every single debilitating detail of my life and hashed over it time and again, all the while stopping myself from living a life of happiness and peace.

I'd chased after love to fill the void I thought only the man of my dreams could fill and suddenly I didn't need it anymore, the void was filled. I felt whole for the first time in my life, I felt healed and finally found the inner peace I'd craved all my life. Calm in my acceptance of everything, what had once caused extreme anxiety no longer affected me. I felt as free as a bird.

Learning to speak my truth and no longer feeling shame in my life were game changers but letting go was my true awakening. My incredible journey of almost ten years led this and I felt like I'd come home... to me.

32: Falling in Love

When I saw you I fell in love,
and you smiled because you knew it.
- **William Shakespeare**

When I look back at the woman I was ten years ago, I see a woman in so much pain, one exhausted trying to be everything for everyone. Out to impress, excite and thrill. Desperate for love, approval and validation. I want to put my arms around her, I want to hug her and tell her she's amazing. I want to tell her to be proud of the life she's achieved, her beautiful children, her amazing family and friends and the fact that she wanted more and got it.

I want to tell her that she's kind and compassionate, that putting the needs of others in front of her own is her biggest strength and beneath her guilt, shame and fear is a strong woman. I wish she'd known how much she was loved and how worthy of that love she was, but then I think, if she knew all that then, I wouldn't be the woman I am today and for that, I am truly grateful.

Today I know I'm loved and I know how worthy of it I am. I've found peace and although my journey is ongoing, the crazy stuff in my head no longer affects me. If situations arise which they often do, instead of my old reactions, something new is available to me. I observe my triggers and make decisions based on facts, not my program of fear. My need for control is gone and my days of being consumed by anxiety are over. My habit of sensationalising drama and sticking my head in the sand to avoid it is broken and I face up to my life and whatever comes with that.

I believe in myself, I know who I am absolutely and without doubt and I'm not afraid anymore. Overcoming my fear has been one of the biggest achievements of my life. Now I shout out my dreams to the world, am free of the need to comply or fit in and offer my opinions, speak my truth and stand up for myself without concerning myself with what people think of me. It's exhilarating and empowering. The true version of me has emerged to take her place at the forefront of my life and I live without reservation, free-spirited and confident, with an optimistic and positive outlook on my life.

In moments of fear and doubt, my anxiety can flare, but moments are usually all they are. I don't unpack my bags and live there anymore. My paradigm has shifted and there's no going back. Every day I grow and evolve and I observe this growth with fascination. Have I really come this far? My non-reaction to things blows my mind, it's like a superpower. I have boundaries in my life, something noticeably missing in the past. I don't explain myself for the decisions I make, I'm more conscientious in everything I do and I completely detach from drama.

I'm no longer in pursuit of everything in my life - happiness, love, money, success. Constantly seeking more was exhausting and although I desire more, I no longer need it to make me happy. I'm already happy and have made peace with who I am. I've made peace with my life.

In the end I found the love I sought since the beginning of time. I found the person who gets me, who allows me to be the best version of myself, who supports and nurtures me, encourages and loves me unconditionally. Who treats me with the utmost respect and cherishes me. I've never felt love like it before and it makes me deliriously happy. We go for long walks together and have amazing conversations about life. We sit in stillness and enjoy a sunset or sit in stillness and enjoy just being together. We do yoga, meditate regularly, laugh, cry, drink wine and dance together.

The person I'm in love with is me. This is real love and the start of everything else in my life...because all love starts with self-love.

By loving myself first, I've realised what love is and of course the Universe responded. My outlook changed and my life clicked into place, my role as a mother is everything to me, my relationships with my family and friends have deeper meaning and my career has taken a huge leap forward. On top of that, I attracted the most beautiful, romantic love into my life. A love that allows me to finally be me with a man who takes my breath away with his humility and kindness, but that's another story and one I'll share very soon.

Namaste
Suzanne
X

About the Author

Born in Dublin in 1972. Suzanne moved to London when she was 20 and has lived there ever since. In her early 20s she married an Englishman and had three sons with him. After 12 years, her marriage came to an end and her journey of self realisation began. Very soon into her journey, she realised she had a voice that people listened to and became a motivational speaker and a motivational writer. She started writing Champagne and Self-Loathing when her marriage ended and finally finished it ten years later. She currently lives in Essex with her three sons.

CPSIA information can be obtained
at www.ICGtesting.com
Printed in the USA
BVHW041945080321
602015BV00011B/91